W9-CHL-957

RADICALLY COMMITTED

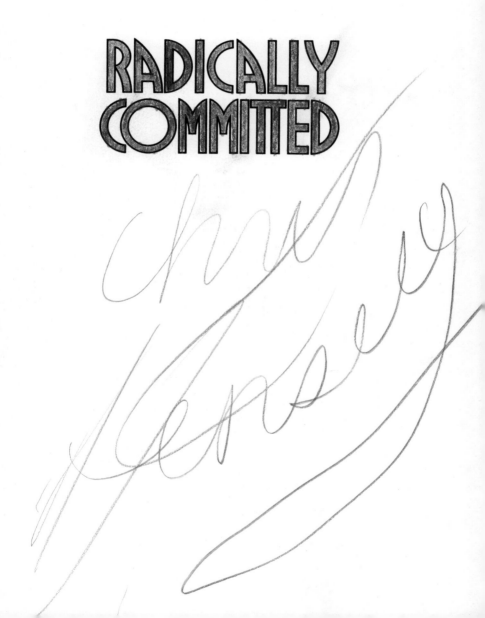

JIM BURNS
RADICALLY COMMITTED

WORD PUBLISHING
Dallas·London·Vancouver·Melbourne

RADICALLY COMMITTED

Copyright © 1991 by Jim Burns. All rights reserved. No portion of
this book may be reproduced in any form, except for brief quotations in reviews, without written permission from the publisher.

Unless otherwise noted, all Scripture quotations in this book are
from The Holy Bible, New International Version. Copyright ©
1973, 1978, 1984 International Bible Society. Used by permission
of Zondervan Bible Publishers.

Library of Congress Cataloging-in-Publication Data

Burns, Jim. 1953–
    Radically committed / by Jim Burns.
      p.   cm.
    ISBN 0–8499–3229–7
    1. Christian leadership   I. Title.
    BV652.1.B86   1991
    253—dc20   91–27425
                                               CIP

Printed in the United States of America
  2 3 4 5 9 LB   9 8 7 6 5 4 3 2 1

To Dale and Karen Walters

You've taught me that
actions speak louder than words.
Thank you for your life style of love,
service, and encouragement. God has used
you greatly in my life and our family's
life. We are most blessed to call
you our friends.

Other Books by Jim Burns

Radical Respect: Healthy Attitudes Towards Love, Sex, and Dating
(Harvest House)

90 Days Through the New Testament (Gospel Light)

Surviving Adolescence (Word Publishing)

Drug Proof Your Kids (coauthor Steve Arterburn; Focus on the Family)

The Youth Builder: Today's Resource for Relational Youth Ministry
(Harvest House)

Getting in Touch with God (Harvest House)

The Youth Worker Book of Case Studies (Gospel Light)

High School Ministry (coauthor Mike Yaconelli; Zondervan Publishing)

Life of Christ Series (Harvest House)

> *The Incredible Christ*
> *The Greatest Stories Ever Told*
> *Getting Your Priorities Straight*
> *Radical for the King*
> *Leader's Guide*

Christian Growth Series (Harvest House)

> *Commitment to Growth*
> *Leader's Guide*

Christian Life Series (Harvest House)

> *Putting God First*
> *Making Your Life Count*
> *Living Your Life . . . as God Intended*
> *Giving Yourself to God*
> *Leader's Guide*

About the Author

Jim Burns is President of the National Institute of Youth Ministry. NIYM is an organization training adults who work most closely with youth to help them make positive decisions during very critical years, and to prevent crisis situations in the home. NIYM holds several youth, youth worker, and parent conferences each year.

For a free information packet about the National Insititue of Youth Ministry, or for information regarding videos, books, or other resources, write to:

The National Insititute of Youth Ministry
P. O. Box 4374
San Clemente, CA 92674
Telephone: (714) 498-4418

CONTENTS

How to Use This Book

From the Editors

Radically Committed is much more than a book. It's a learning experience. Although it's a great book to read alone, it's also written with groups and families in mind.

Included at the end of each chapter is an excellent experiential educational curriculum. It's based on the fact that students learn best through interaction and discussion. After each chapter, Jim has written a "Learning to Lead" curriculum. These sections are divided into five parts. *Things to Think About* provides general questions that will help students clarify the issues and principles in the chapter. *Action Steps* asks students to make practical personal decisions about the issues in the chapter. *Group or Family Experience* ties everything together with group activities that allow students to talk over their feelings and issues with each other and with trusted adults such as parents and youth workers. The *Bible Study* section supplies the practical issues of the chapter with Christian principles directly from Scripture. And the *Related Scripture* section is a list of scriptures that relate to the chapter topic and can help the leader in a further study of the topic from the Bible.

This material has been used with literally thousands of students, parents, and youth workers, and is now available in one easy-to-teach format. The emphasis is on:

- Discussion and interaction
- Goal setting and decision making
- Thinking critically about important issues
- Relating to peers and adults

Radically Committed is designed for a variety of uses:

- *Small group discussion and interaction.* Youth groups can use it as a helpful and lively tool for interaction.
- *Parent/teen discussion.* Many families are now setting aside a weekly "study time" or extended parent/teen weekend to discuss important topics like those found in *Radically Committed.*
- *Retreat and camp formats.* More educational and spiritual commitments can often take place outside the classroom in the non-threatening environment provided at a camp or retreat.
- *Church school and youth group curriculum.* These subjects and chapters have been time-tested to relate to where kids are today. The author has written this curriculum not from an ivory tower but as a person who works with kids in the trenches.
- *Christian school classes.* This is an excellent resource for classes in Bible and Christian leadership.

The companion audiotape and videotape series is also geared toward helping youth interact with peers and adults. It is our prayer that you will find it useful in helping students make a difference in our world.

INTRODUCTION

A group of students were sitting in our living room discussing what they wanted to be when they became adults. It was very inspiring for me to hear that some were already thinking of some excellent careers like medicine, law, ministry, education—the list went on.

One young friend said, "I want to be rich."

"Okay," I said, "but what do you want to be and do with your life?"

"It doesn't really matter," he shot back. "I want to live in a big home overlooking the ocean. I want to drive a Porsche, own a yacht, and have enough money to travel the world."

I smiled and said, "But how do you want to make that money?"

Again he retorted, "It really doesn't matter."

Because we had a good relationship, I thought he could take some prodding; so I said, "I think your goals are far too low. You have incredible leadership ability, and if your only desire in life is to be rich, you can't reach your full potential."

Today that young man is a missionary to some of the poorest of the poor in South America. He doesn't own that home overlooking the ocean, and his Jeep doesn't even resemble a Porsche. But you have to know that his radical commitment has him doing something much greater with his life than just making money. And he is truly happy making a difference in the lives of hundreds of people.

How about you? What do you want to be and do with your life? God has given each of us twenty-four hours a day to live life to the fullest. That's 1,440 minutes, or 86,400 seconds. We can choose to live those hours, minutes, and seconds for ourselves, or to take the courageous step of becoming a true disciple, a radically committed Christian—even a leader among his people. Life's too short to settle for the mundane rather than the miraculous. Life's too short to settle for mediocrity rather than excellence. Life's too short not to make a difference in this world.

This book is intended to challenge young Christians to make their lives count for Christ. You are the salt of the earth. You can make a difference. Committed Christianity is not an easy road, but it's not a boring road, either. There is absolutely nothing more exciting than saying to Jesus, "I'm willing to go anywhere and do anything for you." This book is my attempt to help young Christian leaders grow in discipleship, and develop the leadership qualities required to make a difference in the world.

The great Old Testament prophet Isaiah wrote down this conversation with God several thousand years ago: "Then I heard the voice of the Lord saying, 'Whom shall I send? And who will go for us?' And I said, 'Here am I. Send me!' " (Isa. 6:8).

And then God said: *"Go . . ."*!

I hope that by the end of this journey together you, like Isaiah and so many other "making-a-difference" workers in this world, will also clearly understand the call to Christian leadership and servanthood in your life. *Radically Committed* is dedicated to that purpose.

JIM BURNS

I

Foundations of Commitment

1

CONGRATULATIONS —YOU'RE GIFTED!

Congratulations are in order!

After all, you've got talent. Maybe you've set the pole vault record at your school, or you can play so-and-so's "Fifth Symphony" on the piano—from memory. Or maybe you've memorized the periodic table of elements—in Icelandic. Congratulations!

Then again, maybe you're not so talented. Athletically, you have a tough time clearing the curb; musically, you're still working on "Chopsticks"; and mentally—where's Iceland?

So what? Congratulations are *still* in order! Because even if you're not overly *talented*, you're wonderfully *gifted*.

That's right: every Christian is given spiritual gifts from God. Many people's reaction is, "Gifted? Who, me? You've got to be kidding!" If you're like me, there are many times when you may not feel very gifted . . . but the *fact* is that as a Christian you have received spiritual gifts from a God who *loves* to give gifts!

Your spiritual gifts may be different from those of your friends, your parents, or even your pastor. However, your gifts are important to God. After all, he created you and your special abilities. Every Christian's call in life is to use his or her gifts and abilities for God.

A spiritual gift is a special ability God gives to believers through his Holy Spirit to use for his glory and purpose.

Kim is sixteen. Put her in front of a crowd to speak like her youth pastor and she "dies of stage fright." She doesn't have the gifts of teaching or pastoring. But Kim is an incredible hostess. She loves inviting her youth group to her home, baking cookies, making people feel comfortable in her home and creating a warm, friendly environment. Everyone in the youth group always looks forward to meetings at Kim's home. She definitely has the gift of hospitality.

On the other hand, hospitality isn't Danny's strength. His room is usually a mess. He isn't much of a speaker. He definitely has never been used to heal anyone who is blind. But no one in his family is such an encourager. He is constantly looking for ways to affirm his friends and family. His motto is, "Catch someone doing something right, and tell them." His positive encouragement challenges loads of friends to strive to do better. Danny the encourager is a real leader and positive influence.

The world is a better place because thousands of people use their spiritual gifts to benefit people of planet Earth. Jerry is a missionary. Linda uses her gift of leadership to influence her school and youth group activities. John is not an up-front person, but he has the gift of administration, he's a computer whiz kid, and he has just helped put together the logistics of the summer mission trip. He is using his gifts for good and for God.

How about you? Do you know what your spiritual gifts are? I've listed below all the spiritual gifts found in the Bible, with the five different Scripture references where you can look up these gifts on your own. Place a check by the gifts you think you might have.

Romans 12:6-8 **Ephesians 4:7-8, 11-12**
1 Corinthians 12:4-11 **1 Peter 4:9-11**
1 Corinthians 12:28-30

____ The Gift of Serving
____ The Gift of Helping
____ The Gift of Exhortation
____ The Gift of Giving
____ The Gift of Teaching
____ The Gift of Pastoring
____ The Gift of Mercy
____ The Gift of Hospitality
____ The Gift of Leadership
____ The Gift of Administration
____ The Gift of Wisdom
____ The Gift of Knowledge
____ The Gift of Evangelism
____ The Gift of Prophecy
____ The Gift of Tongues and Interpretation
____ The Gift of Healing
____ The Gift of Miracles
____ The Gift of Faith

The great news is that you don't have to be the most popular person in school to be a leader or to use your spiritual gifts. You don't have to be smart, good looking, rich, or a spiritual giant. God gives everyone gifts, and as you can see there are more gifts than most people ever imagine.

Are you willing to say, "*Use me* today" to God? Are you willing to say, "God, I'm open to whatever gifts you have for me to help make this world a better place?" Are you willing to say, "God, I give you my gifts, my talents and my life?" If your answer is yes, then God will use you in ways you never imagined. Seek his gifts. Search for his purpose. You are on your way to a fulfilled life.

Please never forget:

- You are gifted from God.
- You are an unrepeatable miracle.
- You have gifts and talents that today remain untapped.
- God can and will (if you are willing) use your help to change the world.

Disciplines in Discipleship

Things to Think About

1. How can it be harmful to your faith to wish you had someone else's spiritual gifts?
2. Is the concept of God's having given you spiritual gifts a difficult concept to understand? If so, why?
3. How will your role as a gifted Christian challenge others to use their own gifts and abilities?
4. Read through the parable of the talents in Matthew 25:14-30. How does this story relate to using your God-given gifts for the kingdom of God?
5. Read Colossians 3:17. How does this verse relate to gifts, talents, and abilities God has given you?

Action Steps

1. Read: Romans 12:6-8; 1 Corinthians 12:4-11;

1 Corinthians 12:28-30; Ephesians 4:7-8, 11-12; 1 Peter 4:9-11. Search each gift and ask God to show you what your specific gifts are.

2. This week use one of your spiritual gifts to benefit the kingdom of God.

   What is the spiritual gift? _____

   How will you use it? _____

Group or Family Experience

1. Put a list of the spiritual gifts in front of everyone in your group or family. Have each person identify each other's spiritual gift(s). This can be a good time of affirmation and encouragement.

2. Put specific, practical jobs in the church and family next to each spiritual gift. Then have the members of the group volunteer for specific jobs that match their gifts.

Bible Study

1. Read: Romans 12:6-8; 1 Corinthians 12:4-11; 1 Corinthians 12:28-30; Ephesians 4:7-8, 11-12; 1 Peter 4:9-11.

2. Search each gift, asking God to show you what your specific spiritual gifts might be.

Yes means: I have this gift.

Maybe means: It's quite possible I have this gift or will have it in the future.

Doubtful means: I really don't think I have the gift, but I'm not sure.

Who, me? means: Most likely I don't have this particular gift.

Huh? means: I'm not even sure I know what the gift is, or what it's all about.

	Yes	Maybe	Doubtful	Who, me?	Huh?
Prophecy	——	——	——	——	——
Pastor	——	——	——	——	——
Teaching	——	——	——	——	——
Wisdom	——	——	——	——	——
Knowledge	——	——	——	——	——
Education	——	——	——	——	——
Exhortation	——	——	——	——	——
Discerning of spirits	——	——	——	——	——
Giving	——	——	——	——	——
Helps	——	——	——	——	——
Mercy	——	——	——	——	——
Missionary	——	——	——	——	——
Evangelist	——	——	——	——	——
Hospitality	——	——	——	——	——
Faith	——	——	——	——	——
Leadership	——	——	——	——	——
Administration	——	——	——	——	——
Miracles	——	——	——	——	——
Healing	——	——	——	——	——
Tongues	——	——	——	——	——
Interpretation	——	——	——	——	——
Celebacy	——	——	——	——	——
Intercession	——	——	——	——	——
Martyrdom	——	——	——	——	——
Service	——	——	——	——	——

Related Scripture:

Acts 2:8
1 Corinthians 1:4-7
2 Thessalonians 2:16-17
James 1:16-17
1 John 5:20

2

BUILDING A
SOLID FOUNDATION

*O*ur family lives in a section of California that is prone to devastating mud slides. Year after year I've watched homes worth hundreds of thousands of dollars slide down steep, muddy cliffs when the rain erodes the foundations. You would think we Californians would know better than to build expensive homes on poor foundations, but every year during the rainy season disaster strikes.

Most of us don't have to worry about fancy homes overlooking the blue Pacific with mud slide potential, but we all have mud slides that come into our lives. *No one is exempt from trouble.* Everyone on God's earth goes through numerous crises and struggles in life. The mud slides of life will come your way, and the people who overcome their personal disasters are the ones who prepare for the mud slides *before* they come.

Recently, while I was watching the evening news, an interview with a homeowner named Paul Swanson caught my attention. There had been horrible mud slides in his community and, in a cul-de-sac with fine homes, his house was the only one that remained intact. "Two years before," he told the interviewer, "all of the folks on this block hired an engineer to consult with us. We wanted to know if we should build stronger foundations around our homes. The geological engineer said he would advise us to strengthen our foundations, but that the odds were against a landslide in the area." Mr. Swanson said he was the only one who spent the $20,000 to strengthen the foundation for his half-million dollar home. The others heard the advice and took their chances. The very next year the mud slides destroyed their homes. They gambled and lost.

How you prepare for the mud slides of life will make all the difference in the world when it comes to your quality of life. The best example I can think of is the illustration Jesus gave in the Sermon on the Mount:

> Therefore everyone who hears these words of mine and puts them into practice is like a wise man who built his house on the rock. The rain came down, the streams rose, and the winds blew and beat against that house; yet it did not fall, because it had its foundation on the rock. But everyone who hears these words of mine and does not put them into practice is like a foolish man who built his house on sand. The rain came down, the streams rose, and the winds blew and beat against that house, and it fell with a great crash (Matt. 7:24-27).

Both houses in this illustration were most likely built out of the same materials. The difference was in the foundation. The rain, winds, and floods came to both houses, yet after the storm only the one built on a firm foundation remained.

Some people believe that because they are Christians nothing bad will ever happen to them. Well, I have news for you. It rains on everyone—"the evil and the good" (Matt. 5:45). Bad things happen even to the best of people.

The question that comes to mind is: What is your foundation built on—rock or sand? People who live quality lives tend to take the suggestion of Jesus seriously and build their lives on a firm foundation. Others build their foundation on money, appearance, work, or scores of other idols in our society. You don't have to look far to see the daily hurts, disappointments, and disasters of people who build their lives on the uncertainty of a shifting foundation.

A famous lawyer wrote, "I woke up yesterday and I realized that I had accomplished everything I had ever wanted to accomplish and I'd lost everything I've ever needed." Good insight from a man who had recently taken his life.

In the parable of the two builders, Jesus calls the person wise if he puts this advice into practice and builds his life on a solid foundation. Are you willing to follow his advice? If so, here are four steps to building a firm foundation:

1. START WITH THE RIGHT CORNERSTONE

The cornerstone is the first stone placed in the construction of a building. If you set it right, you can line up every other stone straight. Set it wrong and everything else you do will be crooked. It's an important stone.

Let's get straight to the point: If your life is a building under construction, what is your cornerstone? What is the one thing upon which everything else in your life is based? All of us have a cornerstone in our lives. For some it's money, popularity, a boyfriend or girlfriend, or a job. These things have their place in life, but they don't belong in the cornerstone position. If you want the best in life, you've got to pick a cornerstone that's solid, won't crack or erode, and will last a lifetime. The choice is simple because there's only one cornerstone in the world that meets such stringent specifications: Jesus Christ.

Jesus is also the only cornerstone that comes with a guarantee. Here's what Paul says about it:

> Consequently, you are no longer foreigners and aliens, but fellow citizens with God's people and members of God's household, built on the foundation of the apostles and prophets, with Christ Jesus himself as the chief cornerstone. In him the whole building is joined together and rises to become a holy temple in the Lord. And in him you too are being built together to become a dwelling in which God lives by his Spirit (Eph. 2:19-22).

After a talk I gave on the life of Jesus Christ, a young man came up to me and said, "I've always looked at Jesus as a crutch for weak people." My reply startled him; "He's not a crutch, he's more like an iron lung. He makes the difference." When you commit your life to making Jesus Christ the Lord and cornerstone of your life, you are making a decision to center your life around the person of Jesus Christ. His will becomes your will. You begin to take on the mind and thoughts of Jesus. The hurts and sorrows of life will still be hurled at you but your source of life is not your own; it comes from the power of Christ within you.

If you have never asked Jesus Christ to come into your life and become Savior and Lord of your life, then now is the time. Don't wait another moment. You will never be a Christian leader if you have never given God your life.

Take a few moments in the quiet of your heart and invite Jesus to become your Savior and Lord. You can say something like this:

> Dear Jesus, I invite you into my life. I take you at your word that you will forgive me of all my sins and set me

free. I want you to be Lord and Cornerstone of my life. I need your supernatural help to follow you. Thank you for coming into my life as you have promised. I pray in faith. Amen.

When you ask Jesus Christ to come into your life and be your Savior and Cornerstone, all your problems don't go away, but you have an iron lung who will help you get through the rough spots.

I love the words of this beautiful story called "Footprints."

One night a man had a dream. He dreamed he was walking along the beach with the Lord. Across the sky flashed scenes from his life. For each scene, he noticed two sets of footprints in the sand, one belonging to him, and the other to the Lord.

When the last scene of his life flashed before him, he looked back at the footprints in the sand. He noticed that many times along the path of his life there was only one set of footprints. He also noticed that it happened at the very lowest and saddest times in his life.

This really bothered the man, and he questioned the Lord about it. "Lord, you said that once I decided to follow you, you'd walk with me all the way. But I have noticed that during the most troublesome times in my life, there is only one set of footprints. I don't understand why, when I needed you most, you would leave me."

The Lord replied, "My precious, precious child. I love you and I would never leave you. During your times of trial and suffering, when you see only one set of footprints, it was then that I carried you." (Author unknown.)

2. BUILD YOUR FOUNDATION SLOWLY

Once the cornerstone is set, you can begin adding stones to the foundation, making sure that *each one* is properly lined up with the cornerstone. This takes time. In fact, it takes a *lifetime* to do it right. Building a firm foundation is a lifelong process. Slow, consistent growth is the best way to attain the spiritual and emotional maturity you need as a Christian leader. In our society we seem to have everything we want at our fingertips *instantly*.

We float from one experience to another, from one high to the next. But people who do this in their spiritual lives usually lack the substance and depth they'll need to survive the storms. My dad was most often right when he would lecture us kids, "There are no free rides."

One day when I was in junior high the local high school football coach happened to watch me throw a football. He came up to me and said, "Burns, you've got potential but you're kind of wimpy! If you want to play for me you've got to start working out. Come over to the weight room and we'll get you on a program." Now I didn't like being called a wimp, but I had dreams of being the next great pro quarterback and I figured all I needed was a few muscles.

The very next day I went to the weight room. Most of the students looked like giants. I went over to the bench press and asked how much it weighed. A Goliath of a person said, "Only 175 pounds." As I lay on the bench, he placed the bar on my chest and turned around. I couldn't move the bar. I was sure it was going to crush what little muscle I had. My face was turning red and I couldn't breathe, but muttered a feeble "Hhhhelp!!!" The same football player picked up the weights (with one hand) and set it back on the cross bar. He suggested I start with no weights, just the bar. I bench pressed a twenty-five-pound bar and did a few other exercises and left. That night I stared in the mirror and, to my disappointment, I didn't look any larger. In fact, if you saw my body you'd easily figure out that I didn't spend much more time in the weight room.

My problem was that I wanted instant growth; and it just doesn't happen that way. Remember this: *people who grow quickly tend to fall quickly.* Consistent, steady growth will help you build your firm foundation. Make the goal of your life to build a firm foundation, and then spend the rest of your life attaining that goal.

I like the apostle Paul's philosophy of life:

Not that I have already obtained all this, or have already been made perfect, but I press on to take hold of that for which Christ Jesus took hold of me. Brothers, I do not consider myself yet to have taken hold of it. But one thing I do: Forgetting what is behind and straining toward what is ahead, I press on toward the goal to win the prize for which God has called me heavenward in Christ Jesus (Phil. 3:12-14).

3. BUILD YOUR FOUNDATION DAILY

Because it *does* take so long, it's easy to get distracted from the work of building a foundation.

It was Jesus who said that following his teachings was like building a foundation. He *could* have said that following him was like a day at the beach or a trip to Disneyland. Instead, he said it was *work*. Sometimes work is pleasurable, and sometimes it's . . . well, *work*.

The best way to do the work of building a spiritual foundation is to do it daily. Here's what it takes:

Desire

Developing a spiritual foundation takes *desire*. If you don't have a strong desire to grow in your faith then you'll never do it.

I heard a story once of a young man in the South who came to a southern preacher and said, "Sir, I desire to follow God. What will it take to be a disciple of Jesus?" Following a classical tale, the preacher replied, "You must hunger and thirst after righteousness for then you will be satisfied" (Matt. 5:6). The young seeker said, "What does it mean to hunger and thirst after God?"

At this question the preacher took him out behind the church to a pond and asked him to wade in the water with him. The seeker thought it was an odd request but followed the preacher into the water. The preacher took the young man's hand and put his other hand on his head. He then pushed him under the water.

The boy wondered what was going on when he sensed the preacher was not letting him up. Now all the weight of the preacher was holding the young man under the water. The young man began to panic and to push away, but the preacher's grip was firm. Finally, as he was running out of breath, the boy mustered all his strength, broke the grip of the preacher, and, with every ounce of energy, thrust his body toward the air.

The preacher's response to the young man was simply, "When you hunger and thirst after God like you desired air, you'll be willing to rearrange your priorities to daily walk with your Lord."

Time

There's no such thing as an instant spiritual foundation. Only the daily discipline of spending time with God will do. In my college days I was too busy and overcommitted to take the time for a serious male/female relationship. Then I met Cathy. It was amazing how I was able to rearrange my schedule and priorities to be with her. It's no different with our daily spiritual time with God. When it becomes a priority we will find the time.

Someone slipped me a note one day that read, "God wants your time and attention." When my life gets hectic God gets the short end of the deal. But it takes time and great care to build a foundation that lasts. A question to ask yourself is, "How much of my time and attention do I give to God?" If you have the desire and you are willing to give the time then you've won half the battle.

Now the process of daily spiritual discipline and exercise must take place. As you develop a daily schedule and live out your goals, you'll see noticeable changes in your spiritual life. Here is a principle from the Old Testament that still rings true today:

> Do not let this Book of the Law depart from your mouth; meditate on it day and night, so that you may be careful to do everything written in it. Then you will be prosperous and successful (Josh. 1:8).

According to this verse the formula for a prosperous and successful life depends on your daily discipline of spending time with God through reading his Word, communicating with him, and becoming obedient to his will. The interesting aspect about Christian growth is that you can choose to build a solid foundation through the daily discipline of spending time with God.

4. FOLLOW THE BLUEPRINTS
(Or, Stick to the Plan!)

It's no secret that to build a strong foundation you've got to follow the instructions. Can you imagine building a home without blueprints? But this is exactly what you're doing if you're building your life without following God's instructions.

Jesus got right to the point when he said, "If you love me, you will obey what I command" (John 14:15). The way to build a strong and solid foundation in your life is to obey the commands of Jesus.

Think carefully about these words of Jesus:

Whoever accepts my commandments and *obeys* them, he is the one who loves me. My Father will love him who loves me; I too will love him and *reveal myself to him* (John 14:21, *Good News Bible*, emphasis mine).

If you read this verse carefully you will be introduced to a fascinating principle of God: *If you obey God's commandments you show him you love him; and, in return, he reveals himself to you.* God actually promises to reveal himself to you in great detail through your obedience to him. Sometimes we get the principle backwards: *if* he reveals himself to us, *then* we will obey him. In reality, obedience often comes before revelation.

Maybe it's time for you to take a life inventory: look for areas where you've wandered from God's best for your life. If you need to make some adjustments, now is the time—*before* you find a crack in your foundation.

The winds will blow. The rain will pour. The mud slides will come. Where your life is *after* the storms will depend on how you built your foundation. Build now.

I leave you with three questions:

1. Is your foundation built on Jesus Christ?
2. What would it take for you to develop a deeper relationship with God?

3. Are you willing to make the necessary adjustments in your life to respond to God's call?

Disciplines in Discipleship

Things to Think About

1. If you could do one thing this week to strengthen the foundation of your spiritual life, what would it be?

2. Is your foundation based on Jesus Christ? How do you know?

3. Describe a time in your life when you first started to build your spiritual foundation. What caused you to get serious with God?

4. What are five "foundation crumblers" in your life that you will have to watch out for?

5. Who in your youth group or family helps you strengthen your foundation?

Action Steps

1. Ask a friend, youth leader or family member to hold you accountable for strengthening your spiritual foundation. You may want to meet on a regular basis.

2. Make a commitment to spend time *daily* with God in personal prayer and Bible study. (For ideas and guidelines, see chapter 7 on "Discipline and Prayer.")

Group or Family Experience

1. Invite a construction worker or contractor to come to your group or home. Or, if possible, have your group

take a field trip to a construction site. Ask your guest/host to explain how he lays a foundation for a building. The principles are similar to laying a firm foundation for our spiritual lives. This practical experience can help you understand the important principles in Matthew 7:24-27.

2. As a group, make a human pyramid something like this:

X

XX

XXX

XXXX

You'll soon discover that unless the bottom row of the pyramid is strong, the rest of it will fall. Discuss with the group how building a human pyramid is like building a solid Christian foundation. You might want to assign *a necessary ingredient for spiritual growth* to each person on the pyramid.

Bible Study

Let's take an in-depth Bible study approach to Matthew 7:24-27. Read the Scripture and fill in as many of the questions as possible.

Scripture: Matthew 7:24-27

1. *Who?*
    a. What persons are involved in the verse?
    b. Who wrote it?
    c. Who is it written to or about?
    d. Who does it refer to or mention?
2. *What?*

a. What is taking place?

b. What words are repeated, omitted, or emphasized?

c. What action should be taken?

d. What can I learn about God, Christ, sin, redemption, or man?

3. *Where?*

a. Where is it happening?

b. What places are referred to?

4. *When?*

a. What time of day, year, etc., was it?

b. Look at the timing of a particular event.

5. *Why?*

a. Are there reasons given for actions to be taken?

b. Are there consequences mentioned?

6. *How?*

a. Does it state how something is to be done?

b. Does it state how something was done?

7. *Application*

a. So what?

b. How does this passage apply to my life?

Related Scripture

Psalm 18:1-3
Psalm 119:105
Proverbs 10:25
Isaiah 33:6
Micah 4:2
Matthew 24:35

John 15:5, 7
1 Timothy 6:18, 19
2 Timothy 3:16, 17; 4:7, 8
Hebrews 4:12; 12:1, 2

3

PRIORITIES: DECIDE TO DECIDE

*H*ere's a typical Jim and Cathy Burns date. We give instructions to the baby sitter, kiss the girls, check the wallet for money, pick up the car keys, give more instructions to the baby sitter, kiss the girls again, get in the car, pull out of the driveway, and drive down the street.

I then ask Cathy, "Where do you want to eat?"

"Oh, I really don't care. Where do *you* want to eat?" she replies.

"It doesn't matter."

"Well, what kind of food do you want?"

"How about Mexican food?"

"Not Mexican."

"Do you feel like Italian? Fish? Burgers? How about Chinese food? I know, let's go get a salad."

"I don't want a salad."

"Well, what *do* you want?"

"I don't care."

Sometimes we have to stop the car and *decide to decide*.

THE TROUBLE WITH NOT DECIDING

The problem with this generation of students is not that they make *dumb* decisions, but that they don't make *enough* decisions. This failure leads lots of wonderful, incredible people into big trouble.

It reminds me of a herd of cows grazing on open range. They eat with their heads down, chewing on one clump of grass, then another. When one cow sees a patch of grass off to one side, it moves to it without thinking. From there it moves farther from the herd to get to another clump, then another, and so on, until finally it looks up and says, "Where did everybody go? I'm lost." The cow didn't *decide* to get lost. It got lost because it failed to make *any* decision.

We humans are like that, too. Often we don't *decide* to do bad stuff. We just fail to decide to live for God, and wander into sin as the result. I don't hear students saying, "Hey, let's go do something really evil tonight. Let's break Commandments Three, Seven, and Nine!" What gets them into trouble is when they *fail to decide* to obey God.

If you want to qualify for leadership by staying out of trouble, you've got to *decide to decide*. So what's the decision? To walk with God . . . no matter what the cost?

Before Matthew was a disciple of Jesus he was a sinful tax collector. Jesus walked up to him one day and said, "Follow me." Matthew got up and followed him that day. When Jesus approached the other disciples like Peter, James, and John, he simply said, "Follow me." They followed him. There came a time in their lives when Jesus' call to "Follow me" meant they had to *decide to decide*.

THE HIGH COST OF DECIDING

Jesus is asking you today to follow him. What's your decision? You will say, "Yes, I'll follow," "No," or "Wait." Actually, you only have two choices because "Wait" is the same as "No" when he stands before you waiting for your answer.

There is no doubt about it. There is a cost to following God.

I like this imaginary conversation:

TOM: (Knocks on heaven's door, and an angel opens it.) Hi! My name is Tom. I would like to see the Person in charge, please.

ANGEL: Sure, come on in.

TOM: Look, uh, I know this Guy is really important, but do you think he would see someone like me?

ANGEL: He sees everyone. You can see him any time you'd like.

TOM: Could I see him now?

ANGEL: Go right on in.

TOM: Now?

ANGEL: Yes.

TOM: (Hesitating, then slowly walking in.) Uh, excuse me, my name is Tom. I wondered if I could see you for a few minutes?

GOD: Hello, Tom. My name is God, and I've got all the time you need.

TOM: Well, I'm going to high school right now, and I'm a little confused about what I should do. A couple of my friends say you can help, but they seem just as confused as I am. To be quite honest, I haven't really been impressed by your work. I mean, don't get me wrong, my friends are really good friends, you know, and they really seem to like me, but, they haven't got it so good. Bob, one of my friends, has a dad that is an alcoholic and my other friend's folks are getting a divorce. The crazy thing is my folks are great. I really love them.

Everything's going great . . . except . . . except I can't seem to see the point in life. In spite of all the junk that is happening to my friends, they really seem to be convinced that you are important. So that's why I'm here. I just thought you could give me some pointers. I just feel kinda lost.

GOD: My price is high.

TOM: That's okay, because my folks are pretty well off. What is the cost?

GOD: All.

TOM: *All?*

GOD: Yes, all. Everything.

TOM: Sheesh. Don't you have a layaway plan? Or how about a pay-as-you-go plan. Isn't your profit margin a little out of line?

GOD: Actually, my cost was quite high also . . . ask my Son.

TOM: Well, uh, I think I'll have to wait awhile. I appreciate your taking the time to talk to me, and I'm sure you're worth it. It's just that at my age, it's a little too soon to give up everything. After all, when you're young, that's when the good times happen. Besides, I think I can get what I'm looking for at a much cheaper price.

GOD: Be careful, Tom. The price may be cheaper, but your cost may be much higher than you think.

TOM: Yeah, sure. Well, nice talking to you, God. Maybe I'll see you around some time.

GOD: Yes, Tom . . . and there's no maybe about it.

GETTING YOUR PRIORITIES STRAIGHT

While walking down the famous Hollywood Boulevard a friend of mine noticed this sign in a jewelry store window: WE RENT WEDDING RINGS.

Rent what should be a symbol of lifelong commitment? That sign indicates that there's a shortage of commitment going around today. Never before have there been so many people who are trying to get their priorities straight, but who aren't willing to count the cost of commitment to really make things happen. You can deepen your commitment. You can decide to decide.

I'm afraid too many people approach life the way a boy approached his commitment to God. "I would like to buy $3 worth of God, please. Not enough to explode my soul or disturb my sleep, but just enough to equal a cup of warm milk or a snooze in the sunshine. I don't want enough of Him to make me love a black man or pick beets with a migrant. I want the warmth of the womb, not a new birth. I want a pound of the Eternal in a paper sack. I would like to buy $3 worth of God, please."[1]

Although you will never be perfect, you *can* get your priorities straight. But you'll also have to understand that to get your priorities straight you'll have to choose commitment.

DO YOU *WANT* TO GET YOUR PRIORITIES STRAIGHT?

Many people are like the heavyset man who said, "It's easy to lose weight. I've lost thousands of pounds." Obviously, unless the man had a medical condition that made him fat, his weight problem was because he wasn't willing to commit to a change of life style and habits. If you *want* to change, you can. It's a matter of commitment to your desires.

Jesus had an experience with a sick man in Jerusalem that illustrates the point perfectly. The story is told in the fifth chapter of John. He came to a pool called Bethesda, which was near what was called "the Sheep Gate." There a great number of disabled people used to come for the healing that was thought to be in the water of the pool.

One man who was there had been an invalid for *thirty-eight years*. Every day, probably about the same time each day, he went to be with all his friends who were also sick. My guess is that he wasn't happy about being ill. Maybe after thirty-eight years he had become comfortable with his situation. After all, he had acted like this for a very long time. Then Jesus comes and disturbs his comfortable atmosphere:

> When Jesus saw him lying there and learned that he had been in this condition for a long time, he asked him, "Do you want to get well?" "Sir," the invalid replied, "I have no one to help me into the pool when the water is stirred. While I am trying to get in, someone else goes down ahead of me" (vss. 6-7).

Jesus comes directly to the point and asks the big question: *"Do you want to get well?"* That sounds simple enough. Our first thought would be, "Of course he wants to get well." But notice the man's response. He doesn't answer with a yes or a no. He makes an excuse. I imagine his reply to Jesus was in somewhat of a whiny voice. At any rate, Jesus doesn't take the excuse as an answer. With piercing clarity he looks directly into the man's eyes and says: " 'Get up! Pick up your mat and walk.' At once the man was cured; he picked up his mat and walked" (vss. 8-9).

You and I are a lot like that man. We became very comfortable with our life style. We always mean to make a commitment but we seldom get around to it. Sometimes we are no different than the sick man who made an excuse. "When I get out of school, Lord." "As soon as I break up with my boyfriend or girlfriend." "Next year, Lord."

But Jesus comes to us just as he did to the lame man, asking, "Do you want to get well? Do you really want to get your priorities straight? Now is the time to make your commitment. Pick up your mat and walk—*now*. Don't let another day of excuses get in the way of your progress."

If you really want to get your priorities in order, read on. The advice in this chapter can make a difference in the rest of your life.

FIVE STEPS TO PUTTING GOD FIRST

1. Know What You Want

Maybe you've heard the statement, "He who aims at nothing hits it every time." What are *you* aiming at? Have you ever taken the time to state your life's goal?

Take a moment to think of something you would really like to do. Then write out a clear-cut goal. Here are some examples:

I want to graduate from college four years from today.

I want to read the entire Bible in one year.

I want to go on a short-term mission trip within two years.

Notice these goals are simple and clear. They state exactly *what* you want to do and *when* it will happen.

2. Make a Plan

If a goal is a *destination*, then a plan is the *map* to get you there. Let's pretend your goal is to read the entire Bible in one year. Now you need to *write out a plan* to accomplish your goal. It might look like this:

1. Buy a one-year Bible.
2. Wake up fifteen minutes early each morning to read the verses assigned to that day.
3. Start tomorrow.

Be sure to put your plan on paper. And be realistic with your plan or it will fade easily. For me, a plan that included reading the Bible at 11:30 at night just isn't realistic—I would fall asleep most of the time, and the goal wouldn't be reached.

A good plan also provides for some form of *accountability*. Ask a friend to help you. If your goal is to read the Bible, you could ask someone at your church to check up on you periodically.

Don't pass up this opportunity to write out goals and plans for your own life. After reading this chapter, take a few minutes to put your goals on paper.

3. Commit Your Goals to Jesus

As a Christian, keep your goals committed to your Lord. A good piece of advice for your life is this: "And whatever you do, whether in word or deed, do it all in the name of the Lord Jesus, giving thanks to God the Father through him" (Col. 3:17).

Although I understand the struggle, I don't understand why people don't commit their goals to Jesus. He is the *Lord*. He has the power. He is the Divine Helper. Yet we continue to go on doing it on our own and most often failing! But when you commit your goals to Jesus you can be assured of his desire to help, and his deep concern for your best interests. Why choose to live without the power—the ability to change—that the Lord has given you?

All this reminds me of the story of a farmer and his wife in the panhandle of Texas. This couple had eked out a meager living in the dusty panhandle for thirty years when an impeccably dressed man in a three-piece suit driving a fancy car came to their door. He told the farmer that he had good reason to believe there was a reservoir of oil underneath his property. If the farmer would allow the gentleman the right to drill, perhaps the farmer would become a wealthy man.

But the farmer stated emphatically that he didn't want anyone messing up his property. And he asked the gentleman to leave.

The next year about the same time the gentleman with the nice clothes and another fancy car returned. Again he pleaded with the farmer, and again the farmer said no.

This went on for the next eight years. Life was tough on the farm. During those years the farmer and his wife had to struggle harder than ever to make ends meet. Finally, nine years after the first visit from the oil man, the farmer came down with a disease that put him in the hospital. When the gentleman made his annual visit to plead his case for oil drilling, he spoke to the farmer's wife. Reluctantly she gave permission to drill.

Within a week, huge oil rigs were beginning the process of drilling. The first day nothing happened. The second day was filled with only disappointment and dust. But, as you might have guessed, on the third day, right about noon, great streams of black, bubbly liquid began to shoot high in the air.

The oil man had found "black gold," or "Texas tea." Finally, the farmer and his wife were instantly rich.

You and I have a reservoir of power from the Lord Jesus Christ, the power to change. Make sure you tap into that reservoir of power. Whatever excuse you might have to keep you from committing your life to Christ is not good enough. Why commit to your own mediocre priorities when you can commit to the exciting plans of the Savior and Creator of life?

4. Don't Put Off Important Priorities

Just like the sick man in John 5, we tend to make excuses and put off making important priority decisions. When people are challenged to commit their lives to following the Lordship of Christ, they so often think it is a good idea or even an important one, but they tend to make excuses and put it off. "When I get out of school, then I will make that commitment." "As soon as I'm out of this dating relationship." "When we get married, then I'll give my life to Him." "After we get a house, then I'll quit working so hard and spend more time with the Lord." The excuses go on and on. With important, life-transforming priorities, too many people take the attitude of "put off till tomorrow what you should take care of today." Unfortunately, tomorrow brings yet another excuse.

The next time you're tempted to postpone making important a decision to put God first, remember this story. A vulture was hungry, and while flying over the river he saw an animal carcass floating down the river on a piece of ice. The vulture landed on the ice and began to gorge himself with this delightful meal.

Soon, however, the buzzard looked up to take a breath of air, and noticed that the ice was moving rapidly toward a waterfall that was only a hundred yards away. But instead of flying away he kept eating, while keeping his eye on the waterfall.

At twenty-five yards he decided to take one last bite. Then at ten yards he took one last mouthful. With only feet before he would go over the falls, he finally tried to fly to safety.

Unfortunately, his feet were now frozen to the ice. It was too late to do anything but tumble to his death over the falls.

Don't make excuses and don't put off your important priorities. Countless people have wasted their lives by putting off important, long-term priorities while tending only to urgent short-term ones.

5. Be Willing to Pay the Price

Commitment is costly. It might take some delayed gratification or rearranging of life style priorities. You must *think long-term*. In industry it is the long term goals and objectives that pay the greatest dividends. And the same is true with life.

If you want a good marriage you will have to invest hours and years of constantly working at your marriage. The other option of not working at your marriage is easier in the short haul, but the negative results will also be evident. Success at whatever you endeavor doesn't come easy. You pay a price when you choose commitment and get your priorities straight. But, it's worth it!

Disciplines in Discipleship

Things to Think About

1. Why do you think it's so difficult to put our priorities in order? (In other words, what keeps us from putting God first in our lives?)

2. Why is it important to have goals in your life?

3. Take a moment to write down two each of immediate goals, six-month goals, one-year goals, five-year goals, ten-year goals, and lifelong goals. Share these goals in a small group or with another person.

4. What is the single most difficult priority for you to put in proper order? Why?

5. Describe an experience in your life when you made a major commitment to God.

Action Steps

1. Put in order the ten most important priorities in your life. List them the way you think would best glorify God.

1. _____

   _____

2. _____

   _____

3. _____

   _____

4. _____

   _____

5. _____

   _____

6. _____

   _____

7. _____

   _____

8. _____

_____

9. _____

_____

10. _____

_____

2. What action steps will it take for you to live in a way that is consistent with your priority list?

3. Tell a friend, youth worker, or family member about a commitment you have made this week, and ask them to hold you accountable.

Group or Family Experience

1. Each person in the group is to write out his or her own definition of the word "obedience." Then have the group share their definitions and discuss why obedience is so important to the Christian life. (John 14:21 may help.)

2. What does the following paragraph have to do with deciding to get your priorities straight?

"I would like to buy $3 worth of God, please, not enough to explode my soul or disturb my sleep, but just enough to equal a cup of warm milk or a snooze in the sunshine. I want ecstasy, not transformation; I want the warmth of the womb, not a new birth. I want a pound of the Eternal in a paper sack. I would like to buy $3 worth of God, please."[2]

Bible Study

Scripture: Colossians 3:1-17

Memorize: "And whatever you do, whether in word or deed, do it all in the name of the Lord Jesus, giving thanks to God the Father through him" (Col. 3:17).

Answer the following questions:

1. As Christians, what are we to seek? (Col. 3:1-4)
2. What does it mean to seek the things above?
3. How is Galatians 2:20 similar to Colossians 3:1?
4. Read Colossians 3:5-17.

   a. In verses 5-9, Paul challenges us to put to death, or put away, "whatever belongs to your earthly nature." He then goes on to list them. Which earthly things do you have most trouble with?

   b. In verses 9-10, Paul challenges the believer to put off the old nature with its practices, and put on the *new* nature. List the attributes of the new nature found in verses 12-17.

   Put a mark by three of the attributes of the new nature that you truly desire to work on this week.

Related Scripture

Psalm 119:1-8
Proverbs 16:3, 9
Lamentations 3:25
Matthew 6:24-34
Philippians 3:12-14
James 4:7, 8

---

1. Wilbur Rees, "$3.00 Worth of God," as quoted in *Improving Your Serve* by Charles R. Swindoll (Waco, TX: Word Publishing, 1981), p. 29.
2. Ibid.

4

THE COST OF DISCIPLESHIP

Make no mistake. Radical, total discipleship is a costly goal. True discipleship means that you are no longer in charge—God is. Are you willing to say, "God, I am willing to go anywhere and do anything to serve you"?

Before answering yes too quickly, you must realize something. Total discipleship is not easy. There's no magic prayer or instantaneous change. Rather, it is a lifelong commitment to follow the lordship of Jesus Christ. He is the Master. We are his servants.

There's a word in the New Testament that best describes a disciple of Jesus. In Greek (the language of the New Testament) the word is *doulos*, which can be translated "bond slave." A faithful disciple of Jesus Christ is a slave to God's will.

Let's face it: "slave" is not a pleasant word. But to be a bond slave of Jesus is *the* highest honor in the world. It means that there is nothing more important than your relationship with God: no career, no relationship, no event comes before your relationship with your Lord.

THE TEST OF TRUE DISCIPLESHIP

One of my favorite stories about true discipleship is told by one of my favorite storytellers, Tony Campolo, in his book

You Can Make a Difference. It's about a famous tightrope walker named Blondin. In the 1890s Blondin strung a tight-rope across Niagara Falls, not only to demonstrate his skill but to challenge his audience:

> Before ten thousand screaming people Blondin inched his way from the Canadian side of the falls to the United States side. When he got there the crowd began shouting his name: "Blondin! Blondin! Blondin! Blondin!"
>
> Finally he raised his arms, quieted the crowd, and [how's this for an ego trip?] shouted to them, "I am Blondin! Do you believe in me?" The crowd shouted back, "We believe! We believe! We believe!"
>
> Again he quieted the crowd, and once more he shouted to them, "I'm going back across the tightrope, but this time I'm going to carry someone on my back. Do you believe I can do that?" The crowd yelled, "We believe! We believe!"
>
> He quieted them one more time, and then he said, "Who will be that person?" The crowd went dead. Nothing.
>
> Finally, out of the crowd stepped one man. He climbed on Blondin's shoulders, and for the next three-and-a-half hours, Blondin inched his way back across the tightrope to the Canadian side of the falls.
>
> The point of the story is blatantly clear: Ten thousand people stood there that day chanting, "We believe, we believe!" but only one person really believed. Believing is not just saying, "I accept the fact." Believing is giving your life over into the hands of the one in whom you say you believe.[1]

Unfortunately, the majority of Christians today shout, "I believe," but live their lives as if God makes little or no difference at all. A faithful follower of Jesus Christ does more than shout. He steps out of the crowd and onto the tightrope with Christ.

THE CHOICE IS YOURS!

You had absolutely no part in your birth. No one asked you where you would like to be born, or who your parents would be. You probably won't have much to say about your death, either. Between birth and death, however, you have lots of choices about how you will live your life. The most important of all your choices is whether to be a faithful, committed follower of Jesus Christ.

I know a business person who recently retired. One evening at church he said, "I climbed to the top of the corporate ladder only to find out that my ladder was leaning against the wrong building. I've wasted much of my life on wrong choices. I'm rich, I own a boat, I've traveled the world, but my wife divorced me, my kids hardly speak to me and, until just recently, I've felt far from God. If I could live my life over again I'd give my life to God and let him lead me rather than try to do it alone. I've wasted a lot of important years and now the money and success mean nothing."

I don't want to live my life in vain, only to discover too late that the ladder *I've* been climbing is leaning on the wrong building. I'm not willing to settle for mediocrity. Being a disciple of Jesus *is* the answer.

Let me ask you a few questions. What are you passionately pursuing right now in your life? Have you settled for a comfortable life style as a "not too hot, not too cold" Christian? Or can you say to God, "I'm willing to go anywhere and do anything for you."

One thing about our Lord is that he never minced his words. When he spoke about discipleship, he said what was on his mind loud and clear: *"If anyone would come after me, he must deny himself and take up his cross and follow me"* (Mark 8:34).

This one sentence is the best description of what it means to be a disciple of Jesus Christ. You see, Jesus wanted people to know what they were really getting themselves into when they choose to come after him. He always wanted people to count the cost *before* they made their decision to follow him. Jesus never lured anyone into the kingdom or bribed and conned them with words they wanted to hear. He challenged them to become his disciples, but always left the choice with the individual.

THE DEMANDS OF DISCIPLESHIP

Let's assume Christ's call for total discipleship at least interests you. To help you count the cost, here's what's required of a true disciple.

1. Deny Yourself

As a slave of Jesus, you will not live life on your own. You will choose to consult with Christ on your plans. Since you were "bought at a price" (1 Cor. 6:20), Christ has every right to make demands on your life. You're *his* now.

To understand what that means, look at what Jesus had to say about himself in Mark 8:31:

He then began to teach them that the Son of Man must suffer many things and be rejected by the elders, chief priests and teachers of the law, and then he must be killed and after three days rise again.

Just as Jesus predicted in this prophecy, he *was* rejected. Who were the "elders"? They were the political leaders of the day. He also said he would be rejected by the "chief priests." And shortly after he made this statement the chief priests refused to accept his claims and began their plot against Jesus. And he said he would be rejected by the "teachers of the law." Who were they? They were the people who set the standards for morals and ethics in their community. And of course they also rejected Jesus.

When you deny yourself to follow Jesus you must understand that you are getting involved with a person who butted heads with the religious and political system of his day. Jesus had grave questions about the moral and ethical standards of his day, and about the people who called themselves the teachers of the law.

Do you realize that as you deny yourself and come after Jesus you might begin to have serious differences with the religious leaders of our day? Do you understand that you might be led to question the moral and ethical standards of our culture? If you choose to come after Christ, you are choosing to balk at our society's prevailing attitudes and philosophy. Fundamentally, Jesus was, and is, the rejected Messiah. His followers can expect to be rejected, too (see John 18:18-20). You've got to count the cost of self-denial if you choose to team up with Jesus. Are you willing to make the cause of Christ your overwhelming first love?

2. Take Up Your Cross

To take up your cross means to sacrifice. It means to have the kind of courage displayed by a Christian named Telemachus, in the fourth century.

Telemachus was a monk who had spent most of his life in a remote community that spent its time in prayer and in raising vegetables for the cloister's kitchen. When he was not tending his garden spot, he was fulfilling his vocation of study and prayer.

One day the monk Telemachus felt that the Lord wanted him to go to Rome, the capital of the world, and the biggest, busiest, and wealthiest city in the world. Telemachus had no idea why he should go there, and he was terrified at the thought. But as he prayed, God's directive became clear.

How bewildered the little monk must have been as he set out on the long journey, on foot, over dusty roads, westward, everything he owned on his back. Why was he going? He didn't know. What would he find there? He had no idea. But, obediently, he went.

Telemachus arrived in Rome during a holiday festival. You may know that the Roman rulers kept the ghettos quiet in those days by providing free bread and special entertainment called circuses. When Telemachus arrived, the city was also bustling with excitement over the recent Roman victory over the Goths. In the midst of this jubilant commotion, the monk looked for clues as to why God had brought him there, for he had no other guidance, not even a superior in a religious order to contact.

"Perhaps it is sheer coincidence that I have arrived at this festival time," he thought, "or perhaps God has some special role for me to play."

So Telemachus let the crowds guide him. The streams of humanity soon led him into the Coliseum, where the gladiator contests were to be staged. He could hear the cries of the animals in their cages beneath the floor of the great arena, and the clamor of the contestants preparing to do battle.

The gladiators marched into the arena, saluted the emperor,

and shouted, "We who are about to die salute thee."
Telemachus shuddered. He had never heard of gladiator
games before, but he had a premonition of awful violence.

The crowd had come to cheer men who, for no reason other
than amusement, would murder each other. Human lives were
offered for entertainment. As the monk realized what was
going to happen, he realized he could not sit still and watch
such savagery. Neither could he leave and forget. Suddenly he
jumped to the top of the perimeter wall and cried, "In the
name of Christ, forbear!"

Of course no one paid the slightest heed to the puny voice,
and the fighting began. So Telemachus pattered down the
stone steps and leaped onto the sandy floor of the arena. He
made a comic figure—a scrawny man in a monk's habit
dashing back and forth between muscular, armed athletes.
One gladiator sent him sprawling with a blow from his shield,
directing him back to his seat. It was a rough gesture, though
almost a kind one. The crowds roared.

But Telemachus refused to stop. He rushed into the way of
those trying to fight shouting again, "In the name of Christ,
forbear!" The crowd began to laugh and cheer him on, perhaps thinking that he was part of the entertainment.

Then his movement blocked the vision of one of the
gladiators, who saw a blow coming just in time. Furious
now, the crowd began to cry for the blood of this monk who
dared interrupt their fun. "Run him through!" they
screamed.

The gladiator he had blocked raised his sword and with a
flash of steel struck Telemachus, slashing down across his
chest and into his stomach. The little monk gasped once more,
"In the name of Christ, forbear!"

Then a strange thing occurred. As the two gladiators and
the crowd focused on the still form lying on the suddenly

crimson sand, the arena grew deathly quiet. In the silence, someone in the top tier of the arena got up and walked out. Another followed. All over the arena, spectators began to leave, until the huge stadium was emptied.

There were other forces at work, of course, but that innocent figure lying in the pool of blood crystallized the opposition against men killing each other for the entertainment of the crowds in the Coliseum of Rome. The event the simple monk Telemachus attended was the last gladiatorial contest ever held there.

For Telemachus, taking up the cross meant to die for the cause. For most of us it doesn't mean a martyr's death as much as it means standing up for what is right, and for what honors God. Sometimes I think it would be easier to stand in front of the Roman Coliseum than to stand up for what is right in our own home, community, or school.

I believe God puts a cause in everyone's heart. Your cross may be drunk driving, poverty, abortion, war, refugees, or hundreds of other important causes. My hope is, as you come after Christ, you will be willing to take up his cross and change the world.

3. "Follow Me!"

Jesus said simply, "Follow me." Who are you following? Are you following after your own decisions, or can you say you are a follower of Jesus Christ? Are you willing to *go* wherever Jesus wants you to go? Are you willing to *be* whatever Jesus wants you to be? In essence, to follow Christ means to release your life into his hands and trust that the God who created the universe can do a better job of running your life than you can.

The first day I met my wife Cathy I decided to pursue her. I changed my schedule to work around her schedule. I changed where I sat in the university cafeteria. I schemed to do everything possible to get her to notice me. I daydreamed about her during class, and dreamed about her at night. I was hopelessly in love. In a sense Cathy was my consuming passion. I was willing to do anything for her.

Christ is asking for nothing else when he says, "Follow me." He is calling for you to make him your consuming passion.

A young disciple of communism broke off his engagement with his fiance. He explained why in this letter:

> We communists have a high casualty rate. We are the ones who get shot and hung and ridiculed and fired from our job and in every other way made as uncomfortable as possible. A certain percentage of us get killed or imprisoned. We live in virtual poverty. We turn back to the party every penny we make above what is absolutely necessary to keep us alive. We communists do not have the time or the money for many movies, or concerts, or T-bone steaks, or decent homes, or new cars.
>
> We have been described as fanatics. We are fanatics. Our lives are dominated by one great overshadowing factor: the struggle for world communism. We communists have a philosophy of life which no amount of money can buy. We have a cause to fight for, a definite purpose in life. We subordinate our petty personal selves into a great movement of humanity; and if our personal lives seem hard or our egos appear to suffer through subordination to the party, then we are adequately compensated by the thought that each of us in his small way is contributing to something new and true and better for mankind.

There is one thing in which I am in dead earnest about and that is the communist cause. It is my life, my business, my religion, my hobby, my sweetheart, my wife and my mistress, my breath and meat. I work at it in the daytime and dream of it at night. Its hold on me grows, not lessens, as time goes on; therefore, I cannot carry on a friendship, a love affair, or even a conversation without relating it to this force which both drives and guides my life. I evaluate people, books, ideas, and actions according to how they affect the communist cause, and by their attitude toward it. I've already been in jail because of my ideals, and if necessary I'm ready to go before a firing squad.[2]

Of course, this young man's cause didn't have the eternal benefits of a disciple of Christ. But disciples of Jesus must pursue passionately their relationship with God just as this young communist did with his cause.

Deep down, most people don't want a tame, humdrum, sheltered monotony of faith. They are seeking a thrilling adventure of radical discipleship. To become Christ's disciple means to put God first in your decisions and to become a kingdom person. To become a disciple means to learn of Jesus, to follow his teachings, and, frankly, imitate his life to the best of your ability. Disciples of Jesus begin to think his thoughts and to act as he would act if he were present in bodily form in this world. When you really follow you become not only his servant but his slave. You were bought with a very high price—God hung on a cross. When you come after Jesus your life becomes his life.

Here's how Paul described his discipleship with God:

I have been crucified with Christ and I no longer live, but Christ lives in me. The life I live in the body, I live by faith in the Son of God, who loved me and gave himself for me (Gal. 2:20).

Disciplines in DIscipleship

Things to Think About

1. What are some of the costs of being a disciple of Jesus Christ?
2. What keeps people from getting serious with God?
3. How can faithfulness to God produce a satisfied life?
4. What steps do you need to take to be a better disciple of Jesus?
5. If nothing was holding you back, what would you like to do with your life?

Action Steps

1. Look at this Scripture: "If anyone would come after me, he must deny himself and take up his cross and follow me" (Mark 8:34). Comment about your thoughts, feelings, or commitments about each of these statements:
   a. Deny yourself
   b. Take up your cross
   c. Follow Christ
2. Meet with a mature Christian disciple and leader this week, asking for advice on discipleship.

Group or Family Experience

1. Here's a case study which may open a good group discussion:

Linda was a leader in the youth group. Her faith and her enthusiasm for God and the group had been an inspiration for several years. During her senior year in high school she started to waiver on her life style. Many in the youth group had heard rumors that Linda was experimenting with drugs and alcohol. When it came to sexual purity, her new boyfriend was known around the school as someone who wouldn't take no for an answer. Some of the concerned students in the youth group got together with one of the youth workers to discuss whether Linda should still be in the youth group leadership core.

As a group, pretend that you are a part of the leadership core. Discuss what you would do about Linda.

2. Take a field trip to an inner-city mission organization and observe some of the leadership. Then ask for a meeting with the leadership and interview them on how they chose to serve God in the inner city.

Bible Study

Scripture: Read Matthew 14:22-33.

1. How would you have reacted if you had been in the boat with the disciples and you saw what looked like a ghost walking on the water? Check the answer that best fits you:

___ Frightened

___ Recognized Jesus

___ Doubted my own eyesight

___ Curious

___ Other _____

2. If you had been Peter and Jesus said, "Come," how would you have felt? Do you think you would have stepped out on the water? Why?

3. What did Peter have to do in order not to sink? (See vs. 30.)

Related Scripture:

Matthew 5-7
Mark 12:41-44
Romans 12
James 1:22-25

---

1. Tony Campolo, *You Can Make a Difference* (Waco, TX: Word Books, 1984), p. 14. Used by permission.

2. Quoted in Bill Bright, *Revolution Now* (San Bernardino, CA: Campus Crusade for Christ), pp. 186-187. Used by permission.

II

Traits of the
Radical Christian

5

INTEGRITY:
KNOWING vs. DOING

A great philosopher tells us about a make-believe country where only ducks live. On Sunday morning all the ducks came into church, waddled down the aisle, waddled into their pews and squatted. Then the duck minister came in, took his place behind the pulpit, opened the Duck Bible and read, "Ducks! You have wings, and with wings you can fly like eagles. You can soar into the skies! Ducks! You have wings!" All the ducks yelled, "Amen!" and then they all waddled home.

Many people are exactly like those ducks. They *know* the truth but they don't *act* upon the truth. In other words, they don't have *integrity*.

Here's my definition of integrity: when what you *know* on the inside matches what you *do* on the outside.

It's tough these days to find people of integrity. It seems to be toughest in the business world. One man told me, "If I were totally honest in my business I'd go broke." But it's even getting more difficult in Christian leadership circles to find examples of integrity. We've seen a dramatic increase in deception and corruption among television evangelists, Christian institutions, and notable religious leaders.

I believe God is calling his people back to personal, uncompromising integrity. We are to live out our lives with honesty, consistency, and faithfulness.

There is a fascinating Old Testament book about a young Jewish boy named Daniel who was kidnapped from Israel and forced into a government job in Babylon. In time he became one of the heads of that government because he was a man of integrity.

You probably know the story of Daniel and the lions' den from early religious instruction. But we often forget what he did to get there in the first place:

> It pleased Darius to set over the kingdom a hundred and twenty satraps, to be throughout the whole kingdom; and over them three presidents, of whom Daniel was one, to whom these satraps should give account, so that the king might suffer no loss (Dan. 6:1-2, RSV).

Daniel became one of three presidents of the kingdom—a very responsible position. But then it gets better:

> Then this Daniel became distinguished above all the other presidents and satraps, because an excellent spirit was in him; and the king planned to set him over the whole kingdom (vs. 3).

Another promotion! Of course some of the rulers didn't like the idea that the Jew, Daniel, was picked above all the other leaders to watch over the most powerful country in the world. Now the politics start:

> Then the presidents and the satraps sought to find a ground for complaint against Daniel with regard to the kingdom; but they could find no ground for complaint or

any fault, because he was faithful, and no error or fault was found in him (vs. 4).

The other rulers were corrupt; Daniel alone was a man of complete integrity. These greedy rulers didn't want an honest man to watch over their deeds, so they plotted a way to get rid of Daniel. Here was the royal setup:

> Then these presidents and satraps came by agreement to the king and said to him, "O King Darius, live forever! All the presidents of the kingdom, the prefects and the satraps, the counselors and the governors are agreed that the king should establish an ordinance and enforce an interdict, that whoever makes petition to any god or man for thirty days, except to you, O king, shall be cast into the den of lions. Now, O king, establish the interdict and sign the document, so that it cannot be changed, according to the law of the Medes and the Persians, which cannot be revoked." Therefore King Darius signed the document and interdict (vs. 6-9).

Notice their lie in verse 7: *all* the presidents, prefects and satraps. King Darius presumed that their "all" meant *all.* But Daniel was left out of their discussions. These leaders knew of Daniel's commitment to the God of Israel, and they knew he would never sign such a decree.

When Daniel caught wind of this setup I'm sure he knew his life was in jeopardy. Yet he continued to worship the true God. This is exactly what the other leaders expected to happen, and in fact had hoped for since they sent spies out to observe Daniel. The plan was to approach Darius with the evidence that would take Daniel out of their lives forever:

> When Daniel knew that the document had been signed,

he went to his house where he had windows in his upper chamber open toward Jerusalem; and he got down upon his knees three times a day and prayed and gave thanks before his God, as he had done previously. Then these men came by agreement and found Daniel making petition and supplication before his God. Then they came near and said before the king, concerning the interdict, "O king! Did you not sign an interdict, that any man who makes petition to any god or man within thirty days except to you, O king, shall be cast into the den of lions?" The king answered, "The thing stands fast, according to the law of the Medes and Persians, which cannot be revoked." Then they answered before the king, "That Daniel, who is one of the exiles from Judah, pays no heed to you, O king, or the interdict you have signed, but makes his petition three times a day" (vss. 10-13).

The story is beginning to sound like the latest Hollywood spy thriller, isn't it? Notice that when Darius hears the story he also knows, along with Daniel, that he was set up:

Then the king, when he heard these words, was much distressed, and set his mind to deliver Daniel; and he labored till the sun went down to rescue him (vs. 14).

Most likely on that day Daniel and Darius had a few meetings behind closed doors. I can imagine Darius trying to persuade Daniel to "bow down just one time and it doesn't have to mean you're compromising your religion." Daniel remained uncompromising in his faith: He was willing to suffer the consequences rather than lose his integrity.

You know the rest of the story. Daniel was thrown into a hole filled with lions, but God prevented them from touching him. The next day Darius came to the death trap, observed the miracle, and brought Daniel out. The Bible then makes clear that Daniel prospered during the reign of Darius. *Daniel's integrity brought peace to his life.* By the way, the Bible also says the lions enjoyed a feast that day. Darius threw the other leaders into the lions' waiting claws.

THE ANATOMY OF INTEGRITY

Daniel's integrity is proof of his radical commitment. I find three ingredients to his integrity. If you dare to be a Daniel, you must make these things a part of your life too.

1. Faithfulness

Daniel was a man of faith. He was faithful in his work. When the other leaders tried to find something wrong or crooked with his work, they failed.

Daniel was also faithful to his God. He was willing to take a stand for what he believed to be right. He was trustworthy and he was consistent. *Most often our actions indicate our loyalties.*

The reward for Daniel's faithfulness was that he became head of the kingdom of Babylon and he could be trusted to serve the king. With this trust he was given freedom, and became prosperous himself. One of my student leaders a few years ago came to me frustrated that he was not given more responsibility in our youth program. My concern was that he had "flaked" on numerous occasions with the responsibilities I had already given to him. My response was simply, "When you are faithful in the small things, then God will entrust to you the greater things as well."

I like the proverb that says, "Many a man proclaims his own loyalty, but a faithful man who can find? A righteous man who walks in his integrity—blessed are his sons after him!"(Prov. 20:6, 7, RSV.)

Friends learn through imitation. If your friends constantly hear you hedge on the truth then they will imitate you. When a dad tells his son to lie to the person on the phone and tell him no one's home, then the father is teaching the son an important lesson that the son will imitate. It's an important principle: when you are faithful in the little things you will be entrusted with greater responsibilities.

A few years ago a woman brought her sixteen-year-old daughter in for counseling. The mother was emotionally distraught; she shouted at me, "Your church is failing and you are failing. My daughter has been sleeping with a boy for a year now and coming to your youth group. What's the matter? Don't you teach morals anymore?"

She touched a sore spot because a few weeks before this appointment her daughter had shared some of her family problems with me. So I turned to the mother and said, as calmly and quietly as I could, "Now it's my turn and I want you to listen. It's my understanding that you had a man living with you for six months out of this past year and now you periodically invite men you meet at bars to come home for the night. In fact, I understand that there have been a few nights you haven't bothered to come home, or even to call your children."

I had her attention. I continued, "Perhaps it's time to understand something. Your daughter is only imitating her mother whom she loves deeply. If you want your daughter to have a different relationship with men, why not start with your own life?" The woman's lips began to quiver, and she muttered a "thank you" under her breath as she walked out to do some important thinking.

If you want to be a good influence, remember that the

saying "Don't do as I do, do as I say" is fine—except it doesn't work! Take an inventory of your life, asking the questions, Am I a faithful person? Can I be trusted? How do I measure up in the area of faithfulness? Is my life consistent with my beliefs?

2. An Uncompromising Life Style

I can't think of a more difficult situation than the position Daniel was put in when Darius approached him to hedge on his worship. The situations I find most difficult for me are not the ones when I'm tempted to act out a full-blown lie. The toughest situations are when I can compromise my beliefs without anyone knowing that I did it.

I read four disturbing books last year on what I would call tarnished ministers. All four of the ministers I read about started out with great intentions, high morals, and a desire to be all that God wanted them to be. However, somewhere along the road they began to compromise. At first they cut corners on unimportant aspects of their ministries, but these compromises snowballed into horrible events. For one reason or another these ministers compromised their values, their faith, and even their morals. They were no longer great ministers.

So many of their compromises were in the area of finances. All four of the books talked about gross misappropriation of funds. They also had similar stories about their leader: a charismatic personality with great zeal for serving the kingdom of God is allowed to operate with little accountability. Under the weight of compromise, their home lives began to deteriorate. Marriages were strained, children developed loads of problems—even suicide. Left behind were heaps of broken dreams and bewildered followers.

All these people started out aboveboard, but let the little compromises of life begin to erode their leadership. They weren't evil people. If anything, they started out overly zealous to do good. They were just good people who compromised.

You and I can choose integrity instead of the road of compromise. It is so easy to hedge; but the long-term results of compromise are breakdowns, low self-esteem, embarrassment, and a real loss of leadership.

If you are compromising in your relationships or school, then make a decision to choose an uncompromising life style. It could be the wisest decision of your life. I want to choose integrity. It has cost me money. It has exposed compromising values I didn't know I had, and it has made it more difficult for me in many instances. But the long-term result of my decision is that I am in the process of becoming a healthier person.

3. Purity

It sounds like an old-fashioned word, doesn't it? Even in Christian circles we don't talk much about purity these days. Yet, in Daniel we find that purity of life was essential to living a life of integrity.

I read an interesting story recently of a fellow who went into a chicken franchise store in Long Beach, California, to buy some chicken for himself and the young lady who was with him. When the store's manager handed him his order, he inadvertently gave the fellow the box containing the day's earnings instead of a box of chicken. You see, he was about to make a deposit; and for safety's sake he had put the money in a fried chicken box.

The fellow took what he thought was his box of chicken, returned to the car, and he and the lady drove away to a park to share their lunch. Of course when they opened the box they discovered they had a box full of money.

Now that's a very vulnerable moment for the average individual. But, realizing the mistake that had been made, the man simply got back in his car, returned to the store, and gave the money back.

The manager was elated. He was so pleased that he told the young man, "Stick around. I want to call the newspaper and have them take your picture. You're the most honest guy in town!"

"Oh, no—don't do that!" the fellow protested.

"Why not?" asked the manager.

"Well," said the man, "I'm married, and the woman I'm with is not my wife!"

Now, I think that is a perfect illustration of how on the surface we may appear to be people of integrity, so thoroughly honest we'd give the quarter back at the phone booth . . . but underneath it isn't unusual to find a lot of corruption there. Look far enough, search deep enough, and we can usually find some dirt.

It's extremely difficult to live a life of integrity in our society. It's difficult to be different, and to resist being seduced by the pressure to conform. My hope is that you and I will choose to walk the road of integrity even if no one else around us chooses that path. The goal is to be honest no matter what the cost. When we choose integrity we choose to approach our life, our relationships, and even our faith with uncompromising integrity and purity.

If we are people of integrity, when we have an opportunity to cheat, we won't—even when 55 percent of today's high school students admit to cheating. When it comes to exaggeration, we stick with the truth—even when the little white lie is accepted and even expected.

The result of integrity? Like Daniel, we rise to the top. We decide to fly instead of waddle.

Disciplines in Discipleship

Things to Think About

1. Write out your own definition of integrity, and share some ways you can develop integrity in your own life.

2. Integrity could basically be defined as "walking your talk." If you could pop outside of yourself for a day, in what ways would you see yourself walking your Christian talk? In what way could you make your walk more like your talk?

3. Why does God want us to become men and women of integrity?

4. Read 1 John 1:6. Would you consider this type of person a person of integrity? Why or why not?

5. Why is it so difficult to be people of integrity?

Action Steps

1. Take a personal integrity inventory. List the issues and characteristics in your life which are lacking integrity. Then, beside each one, make a note of how you can improve this quality in your life.

Characteristic	How to Improve
_____	_____
_____	_____

_____   _____

_____   _____

_____   _____

_____   _____

_____   _____

2. If you are not in a support/accountability group, form one this week. (You may need the help of your youth worker, teacher, or parents.)

Group or Family Experience

1. What would you do if . . .

   a. You're sitting at a red light in the left turn lane. Three minutes pass and there is no change in the light. Would you:

      (1) Look for police or oncoming cars, then go?

      (2) Turn right, drive to the nearest left turn, make a U-turn?

      (3) Wait for the light to change?

      (4) Other.

   b. You leave a store and drive halfway home before you realize the clerk overpaid you. Would you:

      (1) Say, "Next time I'll pay it back"?

      (2) Thank God for the financial blessing?

      (3) Turn around and return the money?

      (4) Other.

   c. You are asked to close the store at which you work. The store closes at 10 P.M., but from 8:00 to 9:30, no patrons come. At 9:30 would you:

(1) Close the store early and save the owner money (electricity, pay, etc.?)

(2) Wait until 10 P.M. to close?

(3) Call the owner and ask for permission?

(4) Other.

d. The person of your dreams says yes to your request for a date—at a time when you have a date with someone else. Would you:

(1) Go on the new date, then break up with the girl you were dating?

(2) Call your present date and call it quits before the new date?

(3) Go on the new date and quit calling your present date?

(4) Other.

e. Create your own situation.

2. As a group, come up with a list of twenty people of integrity. Discuss why you view these people as men or women with integrity.

Bible Study

Scripture: Read Daniel 6:1-24.

1. Why was Daniel distinguished above all the other leaders? (vs. 3)

2. What happened when Daniel's fellow leaders tried to find fault in him? (vs. 4)

3. What did Daniel do after King Darius signed the document? (vs. 10)

4. Why do you think the king was distressed when he

heard from the other leaders that Daniel had remained faithful to his God? (vs. 14)

5. What was the king's desire concerning Daniel's life in the lion's den? (vss. 16-18)

6. What was the result of Daniel's integrity and faithfulness to God? (vss. 19-24)

Related Scripture

Job 2:9, 10	Proverbs 19:1
Psalm 18:30	Proverbs 20:7
Psalm 41:12	John 10:9
Proverbs 14:32	John 11:25

6

THANKFULNESS

I learned an important lesson during one of the worst months of my Christian life. I don't think I've ever felt more depressed or farther away from God. I couldn't get a handle on why I was feeling so blah. Cathy was concerned, and she convinced me to make an appointment with my good friend, John, who is a pastor and excellent counselor.

A couple of days later I found myself sitting at lunch with John, pouring out my story and my struggles. John didn't say much, but seemed to be listening intently. When I finished my story, I waited for his response. It didn't come. He paid for the meal, and as we left the restaurant he said simply, "I've got a verse for you." With that, he gave me a napkin with the words "1 Thessalonians 5:18" written on it.

At first I was hurt and frustrated that John would hear my story and think my remedy was found in a single scripture verse. Usually John was an excellent counselor, but this time he blew it. I wanted insight, not a Bible verse. Then, as he pulled into the parking lot to drop me off, John turned off the engine and asked to pray for me. At least he is going to do his pastoral duty, I thought.

John's prayer went something like this: "Lord, thank you for Jim and thank you for these problems he is having. I thank you in advance for hearing and responding to our prayer. We pray with thanksgiving, Amen."

After this "thanksgiving" prayer I was now livid. As I went into my office I thought to myself, Who does he think he is, thanking God for my problems? The nerve of him! Here was one counseling situation that had failed and, in fact, made things worse!

When I arrived home that night Cathy's first question was, "How was your time with John?" She could tell by my tone of voice that it was less than inspiring. She kept prying, and finally got me to take the napkin out of my pocket and give her the scripture reference John had given me. I hadn't bothered to look it up; but Cathy went straight to a Bible and read 1 Thessalonians 5:18 to me: "Give thanks in all circumstances, for this is God's will for you in Christ Jesus."

The scripture only made me more frustrated. This single verse told me that it was God's will for me to be thankful in all circumstances. I told Cathy, "That is not the answer to my depression." But guess what? Morning after morning and evening after evening that verse kept coming back to my mind. And I've learned a few things about thankfulness over the past few years that have absolutely been a life-changing experience for me.

When it comes to this subject I meet two types of people in the world. There are those who are grumblers and complainers, and those who are thankful and grateful. It is interesting to note that almost universally the person who is a complainer is much less happy than the thankful person. If I drew a straight line on a piece of paper and on one end wrote the words GRUMBLER / COMPLAINER and on the other end wrote THANKFUL / GRATEFUL, which end would you be closer to on the continuum? The odds are overwhelming that you can measure your degree of happiness in life by where you place your mark.

In studying thankfulness I've learned a very helpful idea: Thankfulness is a key which unlocks your depressive emotions. You cannot be both thankful and depressed at the same time. They are opposite emotions. You can be sad, hurt, or angered and still be thankful; but you can't be depressed and still be thankful.

Most leaders I know have a profound appreciation for life. They look at a cup half *full*, rather than half empty. They are grateful people; and grateful people are happy people. Their positive attitude and thankful heart make leadership ability contagious. I want to follow someone with a thankful, happy attitude.

Cathy and I have a special friend named Susie Bolte. She is a wild woman! At any moment of the day she is ready for adventure. She isn't necessarily famous. She wouldn't make the finals in the Miss Universe Pageant (although she is beautiful). She's never been to theological school. However, Susie Bolte is one of the most important Christian leaders in our life because her gratitude for life is genuine, and her attitude is positive.

Susie has had many of life's negatives thrown at her, like most of us. But when she's down she doesn't stay down. Her philosophy is "When life gives you a lemon, make lemonade out of it and press on!" We can't make the decision about whether some of life's negative "stuff" is thrown our way; but we can decide to be thankful, even in the midst of a not-so-perfect world.

KEYS TO A THANKFUL HEART

Let me explain my thoughts by giving you three practical points on thankfulness that can transform your life.

1. Thankfulness Is an Attitude

It was the apostle Paul who said that we should "give thanks in all circumstances, for this is God's will for you in Christ Jesus" (1 Thess. 5:18). But for many of us the attitude of thankfulness does not come easy. We've learned from our past to complain our way through most circumstances. My initial reaction to the verse was perhaps similar to yours. Thankfulness is fine when things are going well, but how can it be God's will for me to be thankful for my parents' divorce, war, relationship problems, my grandmother's dying, and everything else that's wrong in the world? Is this verse telling me I should rejoice and be thankful for family problems or hunger or other tragedies in life?

No—if you look closely you'll see that Paul is not telling you to be thankful *for* these things; rather we are to be thankful *in* our circumstances. There is a major difference between being thankful *for* every situation in life and being thankful *in* those situations. God is not asking us to be thankful for negative situations. He is challenging us to find reasons to be thankful even in the worst of struggles.

I came across a little testimony from an elementary school kid who had a cute way of putting bad theology based on his misunderstanding of this verse.

"Yesterday," he said, "I was riding home on the bus and the kid behind me got sick all over the back of my neck and I just said, 'Thank you, Jesus.' When I got home I found my little sister had knocked over the aquarium and left the water running in the bathroom all day and the whole house looked like an ankle-deep goldfish pond, but I just thanked the Lord for it. And then this morning I mistook Dad's Ben Gay ointment for my toothpaste, but I just swallowed hard and said, 'Praise the Lord.' "

Sometimes I'm afraid we act like the little boy because we don't understand the difference between being thankful *for* all circumstances and *in* all circumstances. Thankfulness is an attribute which transcends your circumstances. No matter what your circumstances, I believe there is reason to be thankful in them. Your circumstances may never change, but your attitude toward them can change—and that will make all the difference.

Above the stove in a friend's home is the modern proverb, "I complained because I had no shoes until I met a man who had no feet." We must face the fact that some of our experiences may not be the best. But we can always be thankful for what we do have.

One of my modern-day heroes is Terry Foxe. Terry was a Canadian runner who attempted to run the entire distance from the east coast of Canada to Vancouver, British Columbia, in order to raise money for cancer research. Terry knew the needs of cancer victims intimately because he was one himself—he was running across Canada with an artificial leg. This amputee ran twenty-six miles every day, six days a week, to raise money for cancer.

Terry's enthusiasm and zeal for life caught my attention during his run, and I remember, day after day, seeing him on the news. People, mainly children, would be gathered around him and he would usually be standing in front of a microphone in a park or shopping center or church building. He would often say, "I don't know about tomorrow but I'm thankful for today, and I'm going to make the most of this one day God has given me."

Terry's thankful heart was an inspiration to millions of Canadians and to people all around the world. He died before completing his run. But Terry Foxe was able to run 2,200 miles; and before he died he received the highest civilian medal of honor given by the Canadian government.

Christians have a special reason to adopt the attitude of gratitude, because we know that whatever comes, our times are in God's hands. It was Jesus who said, in effect, "So don't be anxious about tomorrow. God will take care of your tomorrow, too" (see Matt. 6:34).

2. Make Thankfulness a Habit

I'm told it takes three weeks to form a habit, and another three weeks to solidify that habit. If you want to be a Christian leader, make thankfulness a habit.

In my struggle to develop the habit of thankfulness I tried an experiment I called "Thank Therapy." Thank Therapy is simply focusing on the many things in my life for which I can be thankful. The first time I tried it I took out a notebook and wrote at the top, "Twenty Reasons Why I'm Thankful." The first few were easy; but in my depressed emotional state I really struggled to write down twenty reasons why I was thankful. Thank Therapy is an act of the will to concentrate on the good and not the bad.

No matter what your circumstance, you can find reasons to be thankful. Why not take a few minutes, grab a notebook, pen and make your own list of things for which you can be thankful. Recently I spoke to a group of people about what I'd been learning in the area of thankfulness, and I challenged them to make a list. Here are a few things they were thankful for:

Jesus Christ . . . forgiveness and new life . . . parents— their sacrifices and unconditional love . . . glasses—if I didn't wear them I wouldn't be able to see . . . rain—it brings green and freshness to our land . . . health—it's taken for granted . . . a car—it would be a long walk to work!

When you focus on positive things in your life and give thanks for them, the load seems lighter. Make thankfulness a habit in your life and watch good things happen.

3. Christ: the Ultimate Reason for Thankfulness

What a wretched thing it is to call oneself a Christian and yet be a stranger and a grumbling servant in the Father's house. Christians have every reason to be thankful because Jesus Christ was willing to sacrifice his very life in order to set us free from the constraints of sin. Paul explained it this way: "But God demonstrates his own love for us in this: While we were still sinners, Christ died for us" (Rom. 5:8).

With this expression of love we can begin to understand the depth of thankfulness that can transform our hearts. Yes, your circumstances might be difficult. But because you have a Lord who cares for every aspect of your life you can be assured you're not alone in your struggles.

The sacrificial love of God in Jesus Christ helps me focus on how deep and unconditional the love God has for me. As I reread the crucifixion story in the Bible my self-esteem is always given a shot in the arm. My feeling is, He was willing to do that for little ol' me? I must be pretty special to him. I must have worth after all. Make your response to God's sacrificial love one of gratitude. It will put your life and faith in proper perspective.

GRATITUDE CAN SAVE LIVES

Why do Christians especially need to be grateful people? Because gratitude is such a powerful and life-saving emotion that it can actually save the lives of those we influence.

This was illustrated a few years ago when police in New York City were called to a building where a woman was threatening suicide. She was standing on top of a fifty-four-story building ready to jump to her death. The police suicide squad was taking the woman extremely seriously. She didn't look the type, in her expensive dress and distinguished appearance. But every attempt to convince her to get down from the ledge ended in failure. One of the police officers called his pastor to pray. His pastor said he would come right over and see if he could help.

When this wise old minister surveyed the situation, he asked the captain if he might try and get close enough to talk with the woman. The captain shrugged and said, "What do we have to lose?"

But as the pastor started walking toward the woman she screamed as before, "Don't come any closer or I'll jump!"

The minister took a step backward and called out to her, "I'm sorry you believe no one loves you!" This got her attention, and also the attention of the suicide squad because it was such an unorthodox style. The pastor went on to say, "Your grandchildren must never have given you any attention."

At this statement the woman took a step toward the pastor and emphatically replied, "My family loves me and my grandchildren are wonderful. I have eight grandchildren."

The pastor took a step toward her and said, "But then you must be very poor to be so desperate as to jump."

She looked at her plump body and very nice dress and said, "Do I look like I'm in need of a meal? We live near Central Park in a beautiful apartment."

The pastor took another step. He was now within three feet of her. He asked, "Then why do you want to jump and kill yourself?"

Her surprising reply was, *"I don't remember."*

The pastor had helped the woman turn her focus off her problems and on to reasons to be thankful. They continued to talk, and she even showed him pictures of her grandchildren, with lengthy descriptions of each family member. A year later she was a volunteer on a suicide prevention hotline helping people to choose the thankful life. She had learned the secret that thankful people are happy people.

Disciplines in Discipleship

Things to Think About

1. Why do we tend to focus on the negative instead of the positive?
2. List several reasons why thankful people are usually happier people.
3. Why do you think Christmas and Easter are special times of thanksgiving for Christians?
4. How do you think it makes God feel when we are thankful?
5. How do you think it makes God feel when we complain?

Action Steps

1. This week, consciously concentrate on developing an attitude of thankfulness.
2. Make a commitment to read five Psalms and one chapter of Proverbs every day for a month (you'll complete both of those books in the Bible). Look for the number of times you see the writers offer thankfulness and praise to God.

Group or Family Experience

1. Divide your group into smaller groups, if necessary, and write a psalm of thanksgiving and praise. Then have each group share their chorus with the others.

2. Have each person write down twenty reasons why they are thankful. Share these thankful thoughts with each other.

Bible Study

Look up these verses and comment on how they relate to thankfulness:

Psalm 7:17	Psalm 107:1
Psalm 50:4	Psalm 136:1
Psalm 92:1-4	Psalm 138:1
Psalm 100:1-5	1 Thessalonians 5:18

Related Scripture

1 Samuel 12:20-24
Psalm 34:1-4
Psalm 150
Luke 17:11-19
Philippians 4:4-7

7

THE CALL TO DISCIPLINE AND PRAYER

*L*ife was hard for Elaine. She was confined to a wheelchair, and she was poor. The cerebral palsy she lived with had distorted her face and her voice. And yet Elaine was the most radiant woman I had ever met.

As I pushed her in her wheelchair, I leaned over and said, "Elaine, life has been tough for you, hasn't it? How do you make it so beautifully?"

She said, "Jim, stop the wheelchair. I want to sing a song for you." Then, in her not-so-beautiful voice, she sang,

> *Jesus, I love you,*
> *I give you my heart.*
> *I live for you daily,*
> *Each day a new start.*

With tears in my eyes I thought, That's the answer: daily spend time with God.

Over the past twenty years I've tried many daily devotional formulas. I don't need to be convinced of the need for a disciplined daily time with God; yet I still look for the quick fix, the new formula, the easy method to improve my quiet time. I start out with high hopes and large doses of enthusiasm, but after the initial excitement wears off I fade once again into sporadic, on-again, off-again times with the Lord.

A friend of mine once handed me a note he had written which helped me to change my attitude about daily quiet times with God:

> My Dear Child,
>
> I love you. I desire to spend as much time with you as possible. I took great joy in being a part of your creation and your salvation. I consider my sacrifice for you a sign of my significant love for you. Jim, I want the best for you. I believe in you. I look forward to our daily times together. It gives me great pleasure to spend time with you. Don't forget, I'm always with you.
>
> Love,
>
> God

We can spend time with God daily because of an obligation to look good, or to appear spiritual—or because of a sincere desire to know him. Quality time with God does not spring so much from a sense of responsibility as from gratitude for what Christ has done for us.

A wise pastor once asked, "What is so important that you can't spend fifteen minutes a day with God?" The average American spends more than an hour a day dressing and grooming, but can't find a small amount of time to spend with God.

Look at a regular time with God not as a formula to follow but as the enjoyment of a special relationship in which not only do we talk to God, but God speaks to us and guides us into a deeper relationship with himself.

A disciplined daily devotional life is not an option for Christian growth. It's a must. It's also a privilege. We have the opportunity every day to spend time with our Creator and Savior. A daily quiet time with God will transform a life as nothing else can. It takes discipline, but it's always worth it. Paul's advice to Timothy is important, "Discipline yourself for the purpose of godliness" (1 Tim. 4:7, NASB).

This advice is doubly important for any Christian leader. We all have a spiritual bank account, and if we do not attempt to keep it full then we'll go bankrupt, spiritually, and our leadership will be ineffective.

I just bought a bottle of soda pop that had printed on it, in big, bold letters, "No deposit, no return." How true this statement is for those of us who are learning to lead in spiritual matters!

What does it take to develop a more in-depth walk with God?

BUILDING A CONSISTENT TIME WITH GOD

1. Realize Your Need

Spend time with God whether or not you feel like it! On some days we may feel tired or distracted or far from God; but those are the days we need time with him the most.

2. Make a Vow to God

Tell God of your desire to spend time with him, and promise to do so on a daily basis. A vow or promise helps keep us accountable.

3. Make Few Exceptions

Far too often we make excuses, change schedules, or let the interruptions of life dictate our time with God. We can keep our relationship with God as our top priority by making few exceptions to our daily time with Him. I like what Paul said in Colossians 3:17: "Whatever you do, whether in word or deed, do it all in the name of the Lord Jesus, giving thanks to God the Father through him."

4. Develop a Genuine Sense of Expectation

Expect to meet God in a new way each day. Expect God to speak to you in a personal way. And expect to become the person God wants you to be as you daily spend time in his word. Claim the promise found in the book of James: "Come near to God and he will come near to you" (4:8).

5. Set Specific Goals

Find a specific time each day to meet with God. If you get into the habit of meeting with God at a specific time, without interruptions, it will be easier to remain faithful to your commitment.

Find a quiet place to meet with God. Wherever you choose to meet him, be sure that it is a place free of distractions.

Determine what you hope to accomplish during your meeting with God. Do not approach your quiet time in a helter-skelter manner. Quiet time may vary from person to person, but to remain consistent you must find the method that best suits you.

Becoming frustrated by not meeting with God as often as I wanted, and feeling as though I needed a better understanding of Scripture, I put together a personal Bible study and devotional program. My goal was to read through the New Testament in a disciplined, daily way within three-months.

Each day I set aside approximately twenty minutes to read a portion of Scripture, to reflect and pray, then to respond to

God. This three-month experiment in faith was the most effective program of spiritual growth and discipline that I have ever experienced.

INGREDIENTS OF A QUIET TIME

A devotional meeting with God is your personal time with God. It's not necessarily an in-depth Bible study. The purpose is to build a deeper personal relationship with your Creator and Savior. You will want to include these ingredients in a healthy, positive and meaningful quiet time:

1. Bible Reading

"All men are like grass, and all their glory is like the flowers of the field; the grass withers and the flowers fall, but the word of the Lord stands forever" (1 Pet. 1:24-25). Everything in our world will disappear, but the word of God will last forever. The word teaches us about God, his history, and his will for us today. You can use your quiet time to place the word of God in your heart; as the Psalmist said, "I have hidden your word in my heart that I might not sin against you" (Ps. 119:11).

2. Praise

"Let everything that has breath praise the Lord" (Ps. 150:6). Tell God of his greatness and his majestic power. Adore the Lord of lords and King of kings.

3. Thanksgiving

"Give thanks in all circumstances, for this is God's will for you in Christ Jesus" (1 Thess. 5:18). No matter what your situation, no matter what problems you are facing, take time to consider the things in your life for which you can be thankful. Gratitude can help you overcome negative thoughts and emotions.

4. Confession

"If we confess our sins, he is faithful and just and will forgive us our sins and purify us from all unrighteousness" (1 John 1:9). We keep communication with God open when we confess our sins to him. The root of the word for "confession" means "to agree together with." When you confess your sins to God, you are agreeing with him that you have fallen short of the way he wants you to live. You are letting him know that you desire a right relationship with him.

5. Petition

"Ask and it will be given to you; seek and you will find; knock and the door will be opened to you" (Matt. 7:7). This is an important part of your prayer life, but it is not the only part. Too often we rush to God, ask for things, and then rush away. Do pray for your family, your friends, your church, the government, and yourself. Don't be afraid to ask God for specifics, but remember who is Lord in the relationship—God is, not you.

6. Listening

Solomon said, "My son, if you accept my words and store up my commands within you, turning your ear to wisdom and applying your heart to understanding . . . then you will understand the fear of the Lord and find the knowledge of God" (Prov. 2:1, 2, 5). Prayer is two-way communication. When you pray, take time to listen. God is speaking to you.

Write down the thoughts which come to mind. Then test those thoughts through the inner witness of your spirit. Take time to be quiet before the Lord.

I have never met a person who has a regular devotional time who regrets the investment of time and energy. In fact, the people I know with the most vital Christian faith have all built their faith around a consistent time with God. I love the promise in Joshua 1:8: "Do not let this Book of the Law depart from your mouth; meditate on it day and night, so that you may be careful to do everything written in it. Then you will be prosperous and successful."

The result of communicating with God and meditating on his word is a prosperous life and success. I'm not convinced this is about finances so much as it is about a meaningful and abundant life. God will not take away all the pain and hassles of life, but if we stay close to him, he promises to help us walk through the difficult times in life.

Each day God hands each of us twenty-four hours to live life to the fullest. That's 1,440 minutes. When we use at least twenty of those minutes to be with God, the other 1,420 will be far richer.

Disciplines in Discipleship

Things to Think About

1. Name three ways prayer can bring you closer to God.
2. Why is it difficult for most people to have a consistent time of prayer?
3. When have you felt closest to God?
4. Respond to this scripture: "Discipline yourself for the purpose of godliness" (1 Tim. 4:7, NASB).

5. How is prayer different from a face-to-face conversation?

Action Steps

1. Make a commitment to give God a regular time in your daily schedule. When and where?

   When _____

   Where _____

2. Choose a devotional book or Bible study book with which to begin this week.

Group or Family Experience

1. Write a psalm. Psalm-writing is a creative way to: (1) praise God for who and what he is; (2) open up a new avenue of expressing your emotions, thoughts, and feelings before God; (3) learn to worship God through a different medium; (4) challenge each other to search your hearts and minds to better express your love for God; and (5) evaluate your relationship with God— where it has been, where it is now, and where it is going.

   Here are some helpful hints on how to go about writing a psalm:

   a. Be honest with yourself and God. Tell him how you feel about your relationship.

   b. Recall the great things God has done for you in the past.

   c. Be creative! Set the scene for how God helped you out. Use poetry, analogies, and descriptive examples of God's work in your life: "My enemies surrounded me! As the deer longs for the water, so my soul longs for you!" (See Ps. 42:1.)

d. Use your different emotions. Express the sadness, joy, enthusiasm, praise, relief, frustration, thanksgiving, and pain in your life with God.

e. Confess your sins to God through your psalm, and finish the psalm praising God for his unconditional love and forgiveness.

f. Adore God's creation! Go through the uniqueness of every animal and physical element of his creation you can think of, and describe the detail and beauty of each creation. Praise God for his artistry and magnificence.

Share the completed psalms as a group. Be challenged to write a psalm each week recounting the different events, hardships, and victories you have experienced.

2. While in your group, turn off all the lights and spend an hour in prayer. Try the "ACTS" formula, taking fifteen minutes in each area:

Adore or praise God.

Confess (you may choose to do this silently).

Thank God.

Supplication or prayer requests.

This extended time will go much quicker than you realize. Remember, silence is also an important part of prayer; so don't worry if people choose to pray silently.

Bible Study

The most famous prayer in Scripture is what we often call the "Lord's Prayer." Many Christian denominations repeat this prayer every week in their services. The beauty, intensity, and significance of this prayer of Jesus is unequaled in Scripture. Jesus was teaching his disciples to pray, and he told them to use this prayer as an example.

Read Matthew 6:9-13.

1. What is significant about the way Jesus addresses the Father?

2. How did Jesus place his life in the will of the Father?

3. What concerns does Jesus pray about in this prayer?

4. Take a personal and practical approach to this prayer:

    a. What are specific ways you can honor God?

    b. What can you do to make God's will more a part of your life?

    c. Is there someone you need to forgive? How will you do it?

    d. How can you seek God's help in overcoming temptation in your life?

For some, this prayer has become meaningless because they simply repeat it without thinking about the significance of the words. Take a few minutes to paraphrase the words of Jesus in your own words.

Related Scripture

Joshua 1:8	Philippians 4:6
Matthew 7:7, 8	1 Thessalonians 5:17, 18
Romans 8:26	James 5:16

8

A SERVANT'S
HEART

*T*he other day I was driving down the
freeway when I saw a personalized license plate which
read, "ME FIRST." That certainly summarizes the culture
we live in, I thought. It seems that humankind has never
been more preoccupied with personal gratification. Yet as
this generation becomes more and more consumed with
self, the world also becomes a lonelier and more desperate
place to live.

As we get more caught up in an "I" centered attitude, we
continue to spend millions of dollars on tranquilizers for
nervous disorders, aspirin for tension headaches, and psycho-
logical therapy to clear out our minds. But as long as you keep
asking the question, What's in it for me? you'll be unable to
experience true happiness.

On a New York City subway recently, a seventeen-year-old
guy was robbed and then stabbed to death by two thugs.
Eleven people in the subway car observed the incident, but no
one responded—even at the next stop as the young man lay in
a pool of blood.

In Orange County, California, a woman was raped and
brutally beaten. She shrieked and screamed for her very life for
thirty minutes until she was completely hoarse. Thirty-eight

neighbors in her apartment complex heard the cries, and didn't even bother to call the police. She died the next day.

These tragic stories reveal self-centeredness at its worst. But the symptoms of this sickness surround us. So what's the cure? *Put others first.*

THE MASTER'S EXAMPLE

The call of Christ is a call to serve. Jesus gave his disciples a beautifully simple demonstration of what it means to serve others. It's found in the Gospel of John, chapter 13.

> Jesus . . . got up from the table, took off his outer robe, and tied a towel around himself. Then he poured water into a basin and began to wash the disciples' feet and to wipe them with the towel that was tied around him (vss. 3-5, NRSV).

Notice that although Jesus was the disciples' Lord and Master, he took off his outer garment and tied a towel around his waist in order to serve them. This is a strange act for a teacher—then *or* now. In fact, it was too strange for Peter:

> He came to Simon Peter, who said to him, "Lord, are you going to wash my feet?" Jesus answered, "You do not know now what I am doing, but later you will understand." Peter said to him, "You will never wash my feet." Jesus answered, "Unless I wash you, you have no share with me." Simon Peter said to him, "Lord, not my feet only but also my hands and my head!" (vss. 6-9).

After Jesus had washed all the disciples' feet he sat down to explain the demonstration:

"Do you know what I have done to you?" he asked. "You call me Teacher and Lord—and you are right, for that is what I am. So if I, your Lord and Teacher, have washed your feet, you also ought to wash one other's feet. For I have set you an example, that you also should do as I have done to you. Very truly, I tell you, servants are not greater than their master, nor are messengers greater than the one who sent them. If you know these things, you are blessed if you do them" (vss. 12-17).

In this experience Jesus gave all of us a clear message: *serve others*. Notice the promise he makes in his last statement: "If you know these things, you are blessed if you do them." In other words, *Jesus claims that when you follow his example of servanthood you will be happy.*

The Great Paradox

This whole idea of becoming other-centered is a paradox. You usually become unlovable when you *seek* love. Yet when you *give* love, you become loveable and happy. *Self-centered people are basically unhappy.* Other-centered people are basically happy.

In New York City a woman had been moving from doctor to doctor describing her physical ailments. The doctors would give her a thorough examination and yet could find nothing wrong with her. One wise old doctor examined her and then talked with her about her ailments. He told her emphatically that he had the answer to her dilemma. He wrote out on a prescription tablet, *"Do something nice for someone else every day for fourteen days in a row and come back and see me."* He said the prescription would cost $150, but that it had a money back guarantee.

The woman looked at the prescription. "You mean there's no medication?" she asked.

The doctor replied, "That advice is the best medication in the world."

The woman tried the doctor's prescription. On that very evening she baked some cookies and delivered them to the apartment of a lonely senior citizen. The next day she helped another senior citizen with some shopping. She volunteered at her church, ran errands, wrote kind notes, gave phone calls of encouragement, and every day chose to do something nice for someone else. Fourteen days later she walked into the doctor's office a new person—healthier, happier, and more content than she had been in years. She gave the doctor a hug and said, "Thanks for placing some good old fashioned common sense on your prescription pad. I get your message loud and clear."

Too many people today are consumed with their own petty problems. They miss out on the joy of serving. It seems that one of the major complaints in America is money; no one seems to have enough. Many Americans can't seem to get past their financial worries. Yet it's a fact that the clothes you wear in one day cost about the same as what the average Haitian or Ethiopian makes in a year!

Contrary to what some teach, a selfish life style breeds unhappiness. Jesus was right when he said, "For whoever wants to save his life will lose it, but whoever loses his life for me will save it" (Luke 9:24).

HOW TO BE A SERVANT

Every leader must give special attention to becoming a servant. Here are three principles that can help you become more other-centered. As you read, ask yourself this question: How can I apply this principle in my own life now?

1. Actions Speak Louder Than Words

It was the apostle John who said, "Dear children, let us not love in words or tongue but with actions and in truth" (1 John 3:18). Love is a verb; it's something you do. Have you ever heard the phrase, "Your actions are speaking so loud I can't hear a word you are saying"? Well, the opposite is true as well. When people see your actions of love, then they will listen to your words.

I had an unforgettable experience as a senior in high school. Marie had been in my classes since early elementary school, and to my knowledge I had never once spoken to her. In elementary school all my friends would say she had "cooties"—their way of saying she was a nerd. She was very intelligent, but not very attractive; and many of the kids made fun of her. I'm sure this caused her to withdraw and shy away from people even more. Marie lived around the corner from me growing up, but we never once walked home together. In fact, I'm embarrassed to say there were times I would walk to the other side of the street because I didn't want anyone to think I walked home with Marie.

During my senior year some major changes had taken place in my life. I had become a Christian the year before, and during that next year I realized that as a Christian I was to become other-centered. In fact, I was even to love people like Marie.

One day at lunch as I was going to my usual spot to eat with my clique of friends, I walked past Marie, who was eating alone. Something inside compelled me to stop and ask her a question. The look she gave me was startling. I felt that her look was saying, "Why would you, a social snob, talk to me after all these years?" The next day I decided to bring some of my friends together and eat lunch with Marie. As I

look back at the experience, Marie seemed extremely quiet
and introspective. Our little group ended up eating with
Marie for a week, and then we invited her to come to Christian Campus Life Club meeting one evening. She accepted.

I was still embarrassed to be with her alone, so I picked up
another friend, then drove back to my neighborhood to pick
up Marie for the club meeting. And after the meeting I
dropped Marie off before I took the others home. But we kept
eating lunch with her, and for the next few weeks we continued to take her to our club meetings.

One evening after a club meeting I was about to drop Marie
off when another friend in the car asked to be taken home
first. This meant I would take Marie home last. When we
pulled into her driveway she turned the key off and asked with
piercing sternness, "Why are you and your friends doing this
to me?" I stuttered and stammered something about my new
found Christian faith and she blurted out, "No one has ever
eaten lunch with me from the seventh grade until the time you
and your friends sat with me last month." I could not fathom
the thought that here was a person who had eaten alone at
school every day for five and a half years. My experience
in school had been so different.

Eight years after my conversation with Marie I was speaking at a Campus Life camp in Southern California. After my
first talk one of the key girl leaders walked up to me with
young high school girls hanging all around her and said, "Do
you remember me?"

"You look like a girl I knew in high school," I said.

"That's me," she said, "I'm Marie." She was now in charge
of the Women's Ministry for an entire county in Southern
California. She then added, "Thanks for having lunch with
me 'way back then."

I cried. Actions speak louder than words. *Who is the Marie in your life?* Your actions and life style can make the difference.

2. Treat Others as Royalty

As a minister I have the privilege of officiating at a few weddings each year. One point that I share in every wedding is that the couple standing before me should treat each other as royalty. I say to the bride, "Donna, David is God's special gift to you. Cherish that gift and treat David as your king. Honor him." Then I turn to the groom and say, "David, treat Donna as your queen. Honor her; cherish her as God's special gift to you."

Life would be different if we treated people as royalty. The apostle Paul said it best: "Outdo one another in showing honor" (Rom. 12:10, RSV).

One of my goals in life is to try to treat every person I meet as a special child of God. A friend of mine who has very little to do with the Christian faith made an interesting comment about a mutual friend who is a Christian. He said, "I don't know all about his Christian faith but I do know this. He treats me like an honored guest at a party whenever I am with him."

Jesus made a fascinating comment to his disciples one day concerning loving each other. He said:

A new commandment I give to you, that you love one another; even as I have loved you, that you also love one another. By this [love] all men will know that you are my disciples, if you have love for one another (John 13:34-35, RSV).

This commandment implies that the nonbelieving world has the right to judge if there is a God or not partially by the way we love each other. People are drawn to love. Our motive for treating others as royalty should be one of love. I admire Chuck Swindoll's honesty in this statement:

> I'm like James and John. Lord, I size up other people in terms of what they can do for me, how they can further my program, feed my ego, satisfy my needs, give me strategic advantage. I exploit people ostensibly for Your sake, but really for my own sake. Lord, I turn to You to get the inside track and obtain special favors. Your direction for my schemes, Your power for my projects, Your sanction for my ambitions, Your blank check approval for whatever I want. I'm a lot like James and John. And then the prayer, "Change me, Lord. Make me a man or a woman who asks of You and of others, what can I do for you?"[1]

3. You Are the Only Jesus Somebody Knows

I will never forget a chapel experience I had my first year at a Christian college. One day a missionary speaker stood on the platform and I pulled out the latest issue of *Time* magazine to read. I admit it; I didn't give the gentleman a chance. Yet his opening line was thought provoking. He stood in front of the podium, pointed his finger at the crowd and yelled, *"You are the only Jesus somebody knows."*

I smiled and went on thumbing through the magazine when his second statement caught me off guard. He again yelled, "You are the only Jesus somebody knows," pointing his index finger at another person in the audience. He proceeded to repeat that one statement over and over again. On the tenth time, I looked up and he was pointing his finger right at me. I put the magazine down. I don't remember another word he said, but his opening sentence kept churning inside my brain.

In my life, he was right. I had the awesome privilege and responsibility of representing Jesus to many of my friends and family. They weren't attending a church and had never made a commitment to make Jesus Christ their Lord and Savior. They didn't read the Bible and they seldom, if ever, talked about the Christian faith. As if in a very still, small voice God spoke to me and reminded me, "You are the only Jesus somebody knows."

I was told once about an American soldier in Europe after World War II who walked into a doughnut shop and bought his breakfast. When he walked out of the shop he noticed a little boy with his nose pushed up against the window of the little bakery. No doubt the boy was one of the thousands of orphans left after the war.

The soldier walked halfway down the block, then abruptly turned around, went back into the same bakery, bought a dozen doughnuts, and handed the doughnuts to the little orphan boy who still had his nose pressed against the window. The little boy looked at the doughnuts then looked at the man, his eyes as big as saucers. He stared at the soldier intently and said, "Mister, are you God?" The soldier's act of kindness was an act of God in the eyes of the little boy.[2]

The call to Christ is the call to serve. The truly committed Christian often rises to positions of leadership. Did I say *rises?* The truth is that every Christian leader must *stoop* to positions of service. Radical Christianity leads to servanthood.

What can you do today to become a more other-centered person? What are you waiting for?

Disciplines in Discipleship

Things to Think About

1. What are ways you can be a servant . . .

a. In your family?

b. With friends?

c. At school?

d. In your church?

e. In your neighborhood?

2. How can your youth group or family serve your community?

3. In the book of Isaiah, Jesus was called the "Suffering Servant." Why do you think he was called that?

4. Should we go on serving or caring for someone when there is little or no response from them?

5. Why does the philosophy of the world seem to be opposed to the philosophy of Jesus when it comes to the issue of servanthood?

Action Steps

1. List three people God is putting on your heart to serve. What do you plan to do to serve them?

Name	What You Plan to Do
_____	_____
	_____
_____	_____
	_____
_____	_____
	_____

2. Read the Beatitudes of Jesus in Matthew 5:3-12. After reading, think of what you can do in your home and church to be more other-centered. Start today!

Group or Family Experience

1. Read John 13:1-20 together, then have a foot washing service. Take time after the service to talk about the experience.

2. Serve in a rest home, inner-city mission, community center, Christian camp, or homeless ministry; or adopt a service ministry for a year.

Bible Study

Scripture: John 13:1-20

1. Look for all the principles of service in this story and discuss them.

2. What example did Jesus give in verse 15?

3. What is the result of serving according to Jesus (vs. 17)?

4. What's unique about this story?

Related Scripture

Matthew 10:1-42   Mark 10:35-45
Matthew 23:10-12 Luke 22:26,27
Mark 9:33-50   James 4:10

---

1. Charles R. Swindoll, *Improving Your Serve* (Waco, TX: Word Publishing, 1981), pp. 94-95. Used by permission.
2. Ibid., pp. 52-53.

9

TAMING THE TONGUE

Did you know there is a weapon more dangerous than the atom bomb? This weapon has destroyed more people than any gun, knife, or other weapon of destruction invented by humankind. You own this weapon. It's called "a restless evil, full of deadly poison." It's also called your tongue.

No, this chapter isn't on French kissing. It's about something very basic to committed Christianity: what comes out of our mouth. Here's what James has to say about our tongues:

> If anyone considers himself religious and yet does not keep a tight rein on his tongue, he deceives himself [or herself] and his religion is worthless (James 1:26).

Strong words—teaching that basically questions our Christian faith if we use our words to destroy. James goes on to write:

> Likewise the tongue is a small part of the body, but it makes great boasts. Consider what a great forest is set on fire by a small spark. The tongue also is a fire, a world of evil among the parts of the body. It corrupts the

whole person, sets the whole course of his life on fire, and is itself set on fire by hell.

All kinds of animals, birds, reptiles and creatures of the sea are being tamed and have been tamed by man, but no man can tame the tongue. It is a restless evil, full of deadly poison.

With the tongue we praise our Lord and Father, and with it we curse men, who have been made in God's likeness. Out of the same mouth come praise and cursing. My brothers, this should not be (James 3:5-10).

Your words have power. Here are three things your words have the power to do.

1. THE POWER TO DESTROY

If, as James said, your tongue is a deadly weapon, here are a few of the types of ammunition you can shoot with it.

Gossip

There is nothing quite like a juicy piece of gossip to get our attention. It seems that everyone, once in awhile, enjoys hearing the latest trash on another person—especially a person we don't like very much anyway.

There is only one problem with gossip. It's a sin! That's right—when you gossip you are sinning. Even when you disguise your slanderous remarks with concern, prayer requests, or a smile, gossip is nothing less than sin. In the Bible God places the sin of gossip on the same line as sexual perversion and even murder. In a sense, murdering someone with your tongue is very similar to killing them with a weapon.

Think about someone you know who gossips: He most likely has an extremely low self-image. He doesn't like himself so he puts others down with his tongue. *People gossip because they feel inferior.*

Negative Self-Talk

Nicki doesn't like herself. She tells everyone, "I'm ugly." Nicki thinks she's dumb and is always saying, "It doesn't matter how committed I am. I'm a failure." And, chances are, she's right. Her negative self-talk is producing a *self-fulfilling prophecy.*

A self-fulfilling prophecy occurs when you actually *become* the character you've been describing yourself to be. If you tell yourself and others that you are a rotten person, you will usually become a rotten person. If you tell people that you aren't perfect but God is helping you to become a committed Christian, you are on your way to becoming a Christian leader. Negative self-talk has the power to destroy a perfectly normal person who may otherwise have great potential for leadership.

Cutting Remarks

The little phrase "sticks and stones can break my bones, but names will never hurt me" is *wrong*. Broken bones mend; but negative names and biting, cutting remarks often last a lifetime.

When I was in second grade a new kid checked into our class. He was extremely shy, had a speech impediment, and was basically below average in everything from grades to sports to looks. A bunch of us from the "in" group nicknamed him Albert Fruitfly. We laughed at him and made fun of him whenever we thought we could get a laugh out of his unfortunate looks and behavior.

Over the years, with our cutting remarks and critical comments, he began to take on the personality and looks of an "Albert Fruitfly." How unfortunate that a group of second-grade boys with their own set of problems was leading another boy down the path of unhappiness with the power of their cutting words.

Years after high school graduation, I met "Albert" again. Only this time he didn't go by the nickname Albert Fruitfly, and he didn't look at all like our negative description. After high school he left our community, went on to college and developed a new set of friends who didn't view him as an "Albert Fruitfly." In fact, this group of friends helped him become a Christian and gave him a real belief that with God in his life all things were possible. Today he is happily married and works with a church youth group.

Some leaders try to motivate people by putting them down. Even when this seems to work for awhile, I'm convinced that it is simply wrong. When we verbally cut a person, we are stabbing someone who is made in the image of God.

A high school basketball coach, one of these negative motivators, watched his team warming up before a game. They were having a ball; but were they really focusing on how to win? The coach strode out on the court looking for someone—anyone—he might "stab," verbally, to get the others' attention. He walked up to the young man nearest to him and said, "You think you're hot stuff, don't you?"—loud enough for his teammates to hear. "You could care less about winning this game, right?"

The youth stopped dead in his tracks. He was stunned and devastated. Biting his lip, he looked at the floor. The rest of the team knew the coach's criticism was unfair, and they came to their teammate's defense by soundly whipping the other team.

But did this coach really win? Not when you realize that this one cutting remark gave the young man a low self-image that lasted well into his adult years. It contributed to a personality change that went from joyful and unselfconscious to depressive and shy. Leaders cannot afford to lead by harsh criticism.

2. THE POWER TO CHANGE

Words are for building up, not for putting down. Bill Glass tells a great story about Cheryl Prewitt, who was 1980 Miss America. When Cheryl was only four or five years old, she hung around her father's small, country grocery store. Every day when the milkman would come, she would watch him line the display cases with gleaming bottles of milk. And every day he would greet her with, "How's my little Miss America?"

At first Cheryl said she would giggle in embarrassment. But the idea took root in her mind, becoming first a childhood fantasy, then a teenage dream, and finally an actual life goal. The dream became a reality, the goal was reached. And it all began with a word spoken daily, a seed that became imbedded in the subconscious depths of a young, impressionable mind.

Of course God is ultimately the giver of the gifts that enabled Cheryl Prewitt to become Miss America. But wouldn't you like to be a leader with the ability to plant such dreams in the minds of others?

Solomon gives us food for thought in Proverbs 18:21, where he says: "The tongue has the power of life and death, and those who love it will eat its fruit."

Who in your life needs words of encouragement and affirmation? You can change people's lives with affirming words.

3. THE POWER TO PRAISE

Your words have the power to praise God or curse human-kind. James gave us a strong warning, "Out of the same mouth comes praise and cursing." Truly "This should not be"!

If you want to work on taming your tongue, work on spending time daily praising God. Tell him why you think he is awesome. I love the upbeat nature of the very last Psalm:

Praise the Lord. Praise God in his sanctuary; praise him in his mighty heavens. Praise him for his acts of power; praise him for his surpassing greatness. Praise him with the sounding of the trumpet, praise him with the harp and lyre, praise him with tambourine and dancing, praise him with the strings and flute, praise him with the clash of cymbals, praise him with resounding cymbals. Let everything that has breath praise the Lord. Praise the Lord (Ps. 150).

When I'm feeling down, I can't remain low if I take time to praise God. Another Psalm says, "God inhabits our praise!"

I met a woman a few years ago who, at age twenty-seven, was dying of leukemia. She had three beautiful children, her husband had left her for a "healthy younger woman," and she was very poor. Yet, Elizabeth Dulkin was one of the most radiant, beautiful people I have ever encountered. A few months before she died I asked her how she could have such a great attitude about life in the midst of difficult circum-stances. She looked up at me and said:

"Seldom very far from my lips is praise for my Father. My Father loves me, my Father built this earth for me to enjoy, my Father sent his only Son as a baby to die for me so that I can be eternally with my Father. My Father is so good to me. My Father deserves my praise."

Never underestimate the power of what comes out of your mouth. Never forget that you can choose what comes out of your mouth. Your words have power. Our Father deserves that you use your words in his praise.

Disciplines in Discipleship

Things to Think About

1. What makes gossip and put-downs sometimes so enjoyable?
2. What can people do to control their tongue?
3. In what ways are our thought life and what comes out of our mouth similar?
4. Why do you think praise to God is a great way of taming the tongue?
5. When is it most difficult for you to keep your tongue in check?

Action Steps

1. Make *this* week a "Put-down-free" week. Try to make absolutely no cutting remarks for an entire week.
2. Give three people a word of encouragement this week.

Name	What You Will Say
_____	_____
	_____

Name	What You Will Say
_____	_____
	_____
_____	_____
	_____

Group or Family Experience

1. Someone in the group makes up a paragraph about any subject and quietly shares it with one person in the group. That person quietly shares the story with another person until everyone in the group has heard the story. Then, have the last person share what he or she heard. Note how different it is from the original story. This is a good illustration of how gossip can get out of hand.

2. As a group, make a list of all the positive things your words can do. Then make a list of the negative things as well.

Positive	Negative
_____	_____
_____	_____
_____	_____

For the week, focus on your list of the positive things your words can do.

Bible Study

Read each scripture below and have the group interact on how the Bible relates to the topic of taming the tongue:

Proverbs 17:20   James 1:26
Philippians 4:8   James 3:5-10

Related Scripture

Psalm 5:9   Proverbs 12:18
Psalm 34:13   Jeremiah 9:5,8
Proverbs 10:20   Philippians 2:9-11

III

The Life of
Commitment

10

EVANGELISM: A LIFE STYLE OF LOVE

*I*t's only natural that as you grow in your Christian faith, you will want to share the good news of Jesus Christ with your friends and loved ones. At the same time, many Christians feel timid about sharing spiritual things. We're afraid of being put down or being rejected. Sometimes I've been afraid that if I say too much I might embarrass God. So, unfortunately, many of us simply pray for our non-Christian friends and family and seldom talk with them about the Lord.

Let's get two misconceptions cleared up right away. First, witnessing is *not* a certain, prepackaged formula to memorize and spout off, word for word, like a robot. (There are certain witnessing helps and verses you will want to know well, but you don't want to treat anyone like a machine.) Witnessing is meeting people where they are and treating them as special people, the way God would treat them.

The second misconception: you don't have to be *perfect* to witness. The best witnessing takes place when you are open about your hurts, joys, and even your doubts, yet you share what God has done for you in Jesus Christ. People will not be turned off by your weakness and vulnerability. They will be turned off if they can't identify with "Mr." or "Ms. Perfection."

You've probably heard the phrase "Jesus is the answer." As Christians we know that statement to be true. Yet, the unbeliever has usually not even asked the question. Often we are giving the answer to an unasked question.

Someone has well said, that Christians should live such a radiant life that it prompts the question "Why are you the way you are?"—leading to a positive response about what God has done. Nothing is more powerful and contagious than the answer to a sincere question about the source of our quality of life. That's witnessing with a life style of love.

Your life and actions are your greatest witness. *You must earn the right to be heard and to speak the truths of Jesus Christ.* A friend of mine named John Adams has influenced more people than anyone else I know to give their lives to Jesus Christ. Yet, John is one of the more unassuming people in the world. He's just a normal guy with normal looks and intelligence. He works in a normal job, if you call selling doors normal. But when there is a problem or a need, John is always there. He is as busy as any of the rest of us, but he takes the time to serve and show that he cares. He earns the right to be heard.

Also, you don't need to be a dynamic speaker or have an absolutely miraculous testimony to influence people for Jesus Christ. You do need to be a person who, to the best of your ability, loves God, and who, while not perfect, realizes that your life and actions will do much more than words to bring people to know Jesus Christ.

Here are three principles to remember about sharing your faith.

1. LIVE IT

One of the underlying themes of this book is that, as a visably committed Christian, your life is speaking so loudly I can't hear a thing you are saying. One of my favorite pieces of advice comes from Paul, who shared this with the people who lived in Thessalonica:

> We loved you so much that we were delighted to share with you not only the gospel of God but our lives as well, because you had become so dear to us (1 Thess. 2:8).

Yes, we share the gospel with people; but we share our lives as well. That's the way to let people know God cares for them.

Jesus told Peter and Andrew that he would make them "fishers of men." The fishing illustration is perfect for witnessing. When you fish you must put bait on the hook, and wait. As a Christian, your life is the bait that will arouse curiosity. Seldom do you catch fish by harpooning them or waiting for the fish to jump out of the water onto your lap. Get the message?

Here are four questions for you:

1. What if everyone in the world were like you in personality and attitude?

2. How would you like to reproduce what has happened to your faith in the lives of others?

3. Would you like everyone to discover what you have found?

4. If you were arrested for being a Christian, would there be enough evidence to convict you?

Here's a story about living the faith.

A soldier was wounded in battle. A chaplain crept out and did what he could for the wounded man, even staying with him when the remainder of the troops retreated. In the heat of the day the chaplain gave the man water from his own water bottle, while he himself was parched with thirst. In the cold of the night, he covered the wounded man with his own coat, and finally wrapped him up in even more of his own clothes to save him from the cold.

Finally the wounded man looked up at the padre. "Father," he said, "you're a Christian?"

"I try to be," said the padre.

"Then," said the wounded man, "if Christianity makes a man do for another man what you have done for me, tell me about it, because I want it."

The soldier was moved to envy the chaplain's faith not by what he preached, but because he put his faith into action. This is the type of Christian we all need to strive to be. The dying man saw Jesus in the actions of the padre. May God use you and me in a similar manner.

2. CELEBRATE IT

Susie is a party animal. She doesn't drink, smoke, or carouse around, but she is always ready to have a celebration. On a moment's notice you can call her up and say, "Let's have a party," and in the shortest time people are together laughing and enjoying themselves.

Susie is a committed Christian who believes the best way to let her light shine is to enjoy life to the fullest. Almost every week she brings someone to church—someone who comes because they want to meet the source of Susie's happiness. Susie has the attitude Jesus recommended when he said, "Do not worry about tomorrow, for tomorrow will worry about itself. Each day has enough trouble of its own" (Matt. 6:34). Susie lives one day at a time—and celebrates it.

A recent survey said that one out of four people in the United States would come to church on any given Sunday if they were only invited! One of the best ways to get people's attention in this day and age is to let them see that you are a person with a reason to celebrate.

Contemporary Christian musician Randy Stonehill put it this way in one of his songs:

I'm gonna celebrate this heartbeat

'Cause it just might be my last.

Every day is a gift from the Lord on high,

And they all go by so fast.

So many people drifting in a dream,

I only want to live the real thing.

I'm gonna celebrate this heartbeat

And keep movin' on,

Look toward tomorrow 'cause the past is gone.

If I laugh, it's no crime

I've got great news on my mind.

It's a hope that never fades away.

Now I don't understand

All the mysteries of the Master plan,

But I'm sure the Master does,

So that's okay.[1]

3. A LIFE STYLE OF LOVE

Love is the key to effective witness. Who can resist genuine, compassionate, unconditional love? Let's get serious about loving others. Then people will want to become Christians to experience that same kind of love.

Francis of Assisi was a wealthy, high spirited person. He was self-centered and very unhappy. He felt his life was incomplete. Then one day he was riding through the countryside and he met a leper. This leper was ugly and repulsive because of the disease. Something moved Francis to dismount and put his arms around this suffering human being. As he did this act of love, Francis of Assisi said the face of the leper changed to the face of Christ. Francis of Assisi was never the same person.

Witnessing is not a technique. It is a life style of love. When you love someone with the same kind of unconditional love you receive from God, it can't help but make a difference in their life. Is there anything more exciting or rewarding to do with your life than introducing your friends and family members to God the Creator, Savior, and Sustainer of the universe?

Start today!

Disciplines in Discipleship

Things to Think About

1. How can Christians "earn the right" to be heard?
2. Why do we want others to become Christians?
3. In relation to your witness to others, how do you deal with your own personal struggles and failures?
4. What can *you* do to more effectively share your faith?
5. What holds you back from sharing the "good news" with others?

Action Steps

1. Who's on your "love list?" List the names of those to

whom you hope to show the love of God. What will you do and when?

Name	What You Plan to Do	When
_____	_____	_____
_____	_____	_____
_____	_____	_____
_____	_____	_____

2. On a piece of paper write down your personal testimony of how God worked in your life. Do it this week.

Group or Family Experience

1. Take an evangelism class and learn how to properly share your faith with others. Be a counselor at the next evangelistic crusade or program in your community.
2. Watch the movie *Chariots of Fire*, and discuss how Eric shared his faith throughout the entire movie.

Bible Study

Scripture: John 4:1-42

Listed below are seven principles for sharing your faith. In the Scripture story, find where Jesus used all seven of these witnessing principles.

1. Contact others socially.
2. Establish a common interest.
3. Arouse interest.
4. Don't go too far too fast.
5. Don't condemn.

6. Stick with the main issue.

7. Confront directly.

Related Scripture

Matthew 5:13-16   Romans 1:16
John 7:53-8:11   1 Peter 3:13-16
Acts 1:8

---

1. Randy Stonehill, "Celebrate This Heartbeat," Word Records, 1984. Used by permission.

11

WHO WILL SAVE THE CHILDREN?

I wish you could meet Rebecca. She has the biggest, most beautiful brown eyes on planet Earth. Her high cheek bones, long brown hair, and glorious smile would make any eye turn her way. Little Rebecca is eight years old and lives in Guayagil, Ecuador. She is one of those kids you just want to pick up and hug. In fact, during the hour and a half I spent at her school, she held on to me. I let her climb on my back, we held hands, and even when I was speaking to other children, Rebecca never left my side.

Rebecca in Ecuador will never have the same opportunities my Rebecca in Dana Point, California, will have, because Rebecca in Ecuador is pitifully poor. Her smile shows teeth that are already rotten. Her diet consists of one meal a day of rice flavored with onion and, if she's lucky, part of a potato. That's what she eats every day.

As Rebecca gets older, those beautiful brown eyes will dull and her energy will wane. Life will become more difficult. She will probably get sick, or pregnant, in her teenage years and, by the time she is thirty years old, Rebecca will look very, very old and haggard. She *will* be old and haggard.

When I finally pulled her off me and said good-bye, little Rebecca ran alongside our vehicle. I rolled the window down to say one last good-bye and she screamed, "*Jaime, tu eres mi hermano*" (Jim, you are my brother). But I didn't want to be Rebecca's brother. If I were her brother I would have to help her. And what could I possibly do to make a difference?

You and I are lucky. We live in a fairy tale world. Yes, we have our struggles and our pain is very real. But the struggles of two-thirds of the world are different from yours and mine. For the majority of the world our lives are a fairy tale. Their fight is so much more basic.

We forget that we are wealthy. Let's take a wealth quiz.

1. Do you have more than one pair of shoes?
2. Do you have more than one choice about what you will eat for each meal?
3. Do you have access to your own transportation?
4. Do you have more than one pair of underwear?

If you answered yes to three or more of these questions, then by the overall standards of the world you are wealthy.

Fewer than 10 percent of all people who have ever lived on planet Earth are able to answer yes to three or more of those questions at one time in their life. We ask, "Which shoes?" One-third of the world's population would be happy for *any* shoes. We say, "What kind of food do you feel like today?" If the "other third" of the world eat at all, they are grateful to eat the same food every day. At least half of the world walks wherever they go and can only fantasize about having a car.

I have to be honest with you. I am often numb to poverty. I don't see it around me. I don't want to think about it, and I surely don't want to be uncomfortable. After being with some of the poorest of the poor in Ecuador, I wrote in my journal, "This is painful. There is a part of me that wishes I would never have seen these children. They have faces and they have names."

Who will help save these innocent children? The Scripture is clear. Did you know there are more verses in the Bible about helping the poor and oppressed than any other theme in the Scripture?

He who despises his neighbor sins, but blessed is he who is kind to the needy (Prov. 14:21).

He who is kind to the poor lends to the Lord, and he will reward him for what he has done (Prov. 19:17).

From everyone who has been given much, much will be demanded; and from the one who has been entrusted with much, much more will be asked (Luke 12:48).

And here's a very important message from Jesus:

Then the King will say to those on his right, "Come, you who are blessed by my Father; take your inheritance, the kingdom prepared for you since the creation of the world. For I was hungry and you gave me something to eat, I was thirsty and you gave me something to drink, I was a stranger and you invited me in, I needed clothes and you clothed me, I was sick and you looked after me, I was in prison and you came to visit me."

Then the righteous will answer him, "Lord, when did we see you hungry and feed you, or thirsty and give you something to drink? When did we see you a stranger and invite you in, or needing clothes and clothe you? When did we see you sick or in prison and go to visit you?"

The King will reply, "I tell you the truth, whatever you did for one of the least of these brothers of mine, you did for me."

Then he will say to those on his left, "Depart from me,
you who are cursed, into the eternal fire prepared for the
devil and his angels. For I was hungry and you gave me
nothing to eat, I was thirsty and you gave me nothing to
drink, I was a stranger and you did not invite me in, I
needed clothes and you did not clothe me, I was sick
and in prison and you did not look after me."

They also will answer, "Lord, when did we see you
hungry or thirsty or a stranger or needing clothes or sick
or in prison, and did not help you?"

He will reply, "I tell you the truth, whatever you did not
do for one of the least of these, you did not do for me"
(Matt. 25:34-45).

CHRISTIANS MUST TAKE RESPONSIBILITY

Today and every day there are no headlines that proclaim
the fact that 42,000 people will die in the world today and
every day from starvation. That's 42,000 every day! It doesn't
seem fair. It's *not* fair. Can you personally change this statistic
tomorrow? No. Can you personally make a difference? The
answer is yes—especially if you take responsibility as a
Christian leader.

Leaders who are aware of both needs and resources can
point other Christians to responsible ministry that makes a
difference. Before Cathy and I were married, we began to
send $20 a month to help support two precious girls from
India. Our $20 fed them, clothed them, and sent them to a
private school. Today they are both adults with college de-
grees and vibrant faith in Jesus Christ. And we didn't miss
the money. Now our family sponsors Ramiro, an eight-year-
old in the jungle of Ecuador, through a wonderful organization called Compassion International.

Our $21 a month helps provide a balanced diet, clothes, books, and the Christian education Ramiro will need to live an abundant life. We write letters to him, and he writes back. We do the same for our World Vision child, Wawma, in Africa. The Burns family hasn't changed the 42,000-a-day statistic; but we are committed to do our little part.

When confronted with poverty, it is so easy to immediately get overwhelmed and say there is nothing I can do. Most people throw up their hands and take the easy way out which is to do nothing. But I'm reminded of a story about a man who was walking on a beach where literally thousands of starfish had washed up on the sand from an unusually high tide. The starfish were exposed to the sun and would die if not thrown back into the water. The man would walk along the beach and throw as many starfish as he could into the water, but he really wasn't making much of a difference.

A couple walked by and asked the man why he was throwing the starfish back into the water. "We've been watching you and you've hardly made a difference," they said.

The man picked up another starfish, threw it into the water and said, "It made a difference to that one."

You *can* make a difference. It doesn't have to be on a big scale; you can help one hungry kid or one homeless person. Who will save the children? The Bible is clear, "To whom much has been given, much is required" (Luke 12:48).

SERVING THE POOR IS SERVING JESUS

"Whatever you did for one of the least of these brothers of mine, you did for me" (Matt. 25:40).

The Queshawa Indians in the mountains of Ecuador are an exceptionally beautiful people. They have high cheek bones, and other distinct features. They wear colorful beads. And they are extremely poor. Through Compassion International, my friend, Duffy Robbins, and his family sponsor a little boy named Javier in the little village of Octovalo, Ecuador. The Robbins family's $21 a month and periodic letters has given Javier health, Christianity, and education.

Recently we had the opportunity to meet Javier and his family. One of the biggest events of his life was to meet Duffy, his sponsor. When we arrived in Octovalo, fifty kids were waiting for us. They ran up and touched us. Both Duffy and I are bald headed and they loved patting the tops of our heads.

Then, as if on cue, the kids quieted down and Javier's family came through the middle of this group. Mom was carrying a baby, Dad was in his finest clothes (although he was without shoes), Grandma, Grandpa, aunts, uncles, and I don't know how many brothers and sisters—all came around us. They invited us to their home. Duffy and I were the only people wearing shoes as we walked up the mountain to Javier's home.

Their home was made of mud. They cooked in the corner of their one-room hut when it was cold, and there was no ventilation. These people were pitifully poor. No one wore shoes, no one had clean teeth, and, from the looks of what they called a home, there was absolutely no furniture. The picture on the wall was a picture of Duffy's family.

It was stuffy in the room and I thought I might get sick, so I excused myself. I walked outside thinking about all this poverty. I started to feel angry and a little hopeless. I sat down on a rock, looked toward the heavens and asked God, "Where is Jesus in the midst of their poverty?" And as clear as if it were yesterday I heard a strong, clear voice say, "Jesus is on the face of Javier." When we serve the poor we serve Jesus.

The death rate of children in third-world countries is extremely high. Many mothers in Haiti don't name their babies until they are age five. When a mother was asked why, she replied, "It's much less painful to bury a child without a name."

The call to Christ is the call to serve the poor and oppressed. Every committed Christian in our world must ask, "What am I doing to help my less fortunate brothers and sisters? What am I doing to lead others to help?"

What can you do?

A. *Give yourself to the poor*
  • Help house the homeless
  • Visit widows and orphans
  • Take a short-term mission trip
  • Read books on world hunger and poverty
  • Do a Bible study on the single-most-often-talked-about subject in the entire Bible—poverty

B. *Give your time*
  • Volunteer with a service organization
  • Adopt a poor family in your area to visit and support
  • Teach English as a second language
  • Coach a kid's sports team
  • Plan a Vacation Bible School for latch-key kids

C. *Give your money*

  A wise person once told me, "You are truly converted when your pocket book is also converted."
  • Sponsor a Compassion International child for $21 a month. (For more information on Compassion International use the sheet in the back of this book.)

- Get your youth group, family, or friends to help sponsor hungry kids
- Provide a scholarship for poor kids to go to a Christian camp
- Work one day a month fighting poverty, and donate the money to your favorite service program

Disciplines in Discipleship

Things to Think About

1. What can you do to become more concerned for the world's needs?
2. Why is it sometimes hard to give?
3. What do you think is meant by the term "world Christian"?
4. What are some ways you can relate to the needy in your daily life in ways that follow the example of Jesus?
5. Have you ever personally considered becoming a missionary? Why or why not?

Action Steps

1. Sponsor a child through a reputable relief agency that helps hungry and needy children in the third world.
2. Make a decision to go on a short-term mission experience within the next year. If you have questions, contact your pastor, youth worker, or Christian teacher.

Group or Family Experience

1. Imagine yourself on the other side of the world, and picture what life would be like with open sewers, starvation, war, and disease. Now imagine you've just returned. What are you going to do about all the awful things you have seen and experienced? As a group discuss this experience.

2. Compassion International has put together an excellent resource packet complete with Bible studies, tapes, posters, videos, and group experiences. The "Compassion Project" resource packet is free. You can receive it by writing, calling, or filling out the information sheet in the back of this book. Contact:

   > Compassion International
   > 3955 Cragwood Drive
   > P. O. Box 7000
   > Colorado Springs, CO 80933
   > 800/336-7676

Bible Study

Scripture: Matthew 25:31-46

1. *God wants us to help in the simple things.*

   a. List the specific actions Jesus mentions in this passage of Scripture. Then make your own list of other simple ways to serve.

   Scripture List

   _____

   _____

   _____

   _____

Your List

_____

_____

_____

_____

_____

   b. Why does God want us to serve in the simple things?

2. *True giving is with no strings attached. We should give for the sake of giving.*

   a. What was the attitude of the people—

      In verse 44?

      In verse 37?

   b. What do you think it means to be generous?

3. *Serving people means serving Jesus.*

   a. What point is Jesus making in verse 40?

   b. Have you ever felt as though by helping another person you were helping Jesus? If yes, when and how?

Related Scripture:

Matthew 5:13-16
Matthew 10:42
Matthew 28:19, 20
John 3:16
Acts 1:8
1 Timothy 2:3, 4

12

BE A BOOSTER

Years ago there was a television show called "Topper." It was a zany show but, growing up, I loved it. I still remember one of the episodes, and I chuckle when I think of it.

Mrs. Topper wanted to train her husband to be nicer to her. She found a book titled *How to Train Puppies*, and followed it exactly by substituting her husband's name for the puppy. So any time her husband Topper would do something nice for her, she would praise him and give him a treat. She would rub his neck like the book said to do for a puppy, and old Topper would respond!

Things were going along great until one afternoon Topper found the puppy training book and read Mrs. Topper's notes in the book. Of course, disaster struck the Topper home. He didn't like the idea of being trained like a dog, so he immediately went back to his old ways.

Yet, a major lesson was learned: there is power in encouragement. Whether it's with puppies, children, or grown-ups, you can make a very important, positive impact in their lives through encouragement.

FROM SIMON TO "THE ROCK"

Jesus understood the power of encouragement. He had the ability to draw out the best in people. Remember when he met a clumsy, big-mouthed fisherman named Simon? He looked straight into Simon's eyes and said something like, "So you are Simon the son of John?" Simon nodded. Then Jesus said, "You shall be called Peter" (see John 1:42). Jesus nicknamed him Peter which means "The Rock."

Peter's friends and family probably laughed at the new name Jesus gave him. Apparently he had anything but a "rock" of a personality. His friends and family would have never believed that this uneducated fisherman would some-day be a leader of the Christian church.

Jesus saw beyond Peter's problems, beyond his personality quirks, and beyond his sin. Jesus turned Peter's weaknesses into his strengths. He believed in Peter, and he had the power to draw out his best. Peter changed. It took years, but in the New Testament we see a man who was transformed by the power of God—because Jesus encouraged him.

It's important for you to know that God encourages you as he encouraged Peter and other Bible characters. He loves you, he believes in you, and he can draw out the best in you! He sees you not only for who you are but for who you can become. When we use this same ministry of en-couragement Jesus used, then we can help others to change as we ourselves change. Think of someone who needs an extra amount of encouragement. Give him a dose of love and support.

ENCOURAGEMENT CHANGES PEOPLE

You have the power to affect lives by the way you believe in people. Because God loves you, as a Christian you can believe in others. I love what Louis Fisher wrote about one of the world's great religious leaders: "He refused to see the bad in people. He often changed human beings by regarding them not as what they were but as though they were what they wished to be."[1]

Believe in people and they will respond to your support. Do you know anyone who has a poor self-image, or has had a particularly difficult year? Make an effort to believe in him, and you'll see change.

While in graduate school in Princeton, New Jersey, I worked as a chaplain at a prison. As I counseled with men who were incarcerated for every crime imaginable, I kept hearing the same story over and over again: "No one cares about me out there. No one took the time to believe in me." Some of these men actually didn't want to leave prison because they had no one who believed in them outside those dreary walls.

After a day at the prison I would travel back to Princeton and visit with highly successful students who knew where they were going in life. The major difference was that so many of these students had family and friends who believed in them. What a stark contrast.

Jesus took Simon Peter and patiently believed in him. Even three years later when Peter so blatantly denied him, Jesus stood by him, and Peter changed.

Who is the Simon Peter in your life? What steps are you taking to make a difference in his life?

SHOWER THEM WITH PRAISE

It was Mark Twain who said, "I can live two months on one good compliment." People respond to praise. In a world where criticism and negative statements are a dime a dozen, the people around you are hungry for praise. A basic psychology class taught me that it takes nine encouraging statements to make up for one critical comment.

I was talking with a sixteen-year-old who, on her last report card, received five A's and one B-minus. Even with a successful report card she felt dejected because her parents' only comment was, "You should have gotten all A's." Her parents made a mistake. They should have praised her for her excellent work. People respond to praise much better than to criticism.

Be generous with your praise. A woman named Gail had a son in my youth group. Gail was a note writer. It seemed that for almost any occasion I would receive a note from Gail. She not only remembered birthdays, anniversaries, and holidays; she wrote notes after my sermons or before a vacation. It's funny, but after eight years I still remember some of her words of encouragement, and I've kept her notes. Gail had a wonderful ministry to me through her encouraging notes. You can do the same. Make a list today of ways you can praise others and be an encouragement to them and then start giving.

BE AVAILABLE

I think Jesus had a profound effect on the children who knew him. The Bible doesn't say much about Jesus and his ministry to children, but we do get some insight in one episode in particular. Parents were bringing little children to Jesus. His disciples were very upset at this inconvenience, and they rebuked the parents. After all, Jesus was a busy and important man. But Jesus overruled his disciples and said, "Let the little children come to me, and do not hinder them, for the kingdom of heaven belongs to such as these" (Matt. 19:14).

Jesus took time to be with little children, and the children must have loved him and responded to him. People knew he was available to be with them and heal their needs. And when he was available he was *very* available (although I believe the reason he could be so available was because he had also taken time away to gain strength from the Father). Knowing that you are available to your friends and family may be all the encouragement they need to cope with life. (And if you choose to be available, choose also to take time to refresh your spirit.)

The average father in America communicates with his children less than three minutes a day. What a horrible statistic! How can children grow up feeling loved and encouraged when Dad is seldom around to give them any attention?

My dad was different. Oh, he worked long, hard hours, but he always rearranged his schedule to make it to my athletic events and anything else I was doing. I knew at home he was available if I needed him. I didn't use him as much as I could have, but even knowing he was available gave me a sense of security. It's been years and years since I lived under the same roof as Dad, but even today in his retirement I feel that if I had a problem I could call and he would help in any way he could. That security is stronger than any life insurance policy, and to this day it gives me great reassurance to face the obstacles of life.

Do the people around you know you are available to them? If not, tell them. In fact, maybe you just *think* they think you are available. Tell them again.

Never get so busy or preoccupied that you miss what some have called the "divine interruption." That's when God gives you the opportunity to help and serve one of his children. Maybe someone is lonely, and needs to talk. Maybe someone needs your encouragement. Look for divine interruptions. God will give them to you—but only if you're available.

GIVE THE GIFT OF YOUR TIME

There's not a better gift to anyone than your time and attention. A friend was telling me how his grandmother was getting old and senile. One time at a family gathering she blurted out, "I'm so old, I'm useless. I wish I were dead." My friend turned to her and said, "Granny, your very presence in this room makes a difference in my life."

Don't wait for others to come your way. Drop by a lonely neighbor, a friend, or a family member and give him some of your precious time. Clean out your parents' garage on a Saturday when you could have done something else. The gift you'll give them is much more than a clean garage.

Become an encourager. You can make a difference in someone's life. And guess what? Your encouragement will also make a difference in your own life. Don't wait another day to give this gift.

Disciplines in Discipleship

Things to Think About

1. Who is the greatest encouragement to your life? Why?
2. Why is it sometimes easier to nag than to encourage?
3. What can you do to have a ministry of encouragement to your family and friends? To your youth group? To a stranger?
4. What are some ways you could encourage God?
5. Who do you know who needs your encouragement?

Action Steps

1. Choose three people you will encourage this week:

Name	What Will You Do?
_____	_____
_____	_____
_____	_____

2. Anonymously, send a note of encouragement to some-one this week. Part of your blessing will be *not* to let them know it came from you.

Group or Family Experience

1. *Affirmation Bombardment Exercise.* Each person in the group or family writes down an encouraging word about each of the other persons in the group. Then select one person at a time and bombard him or her with these words of encouragement.

2. Take time to write a parent, brother, sister, grandparent, friend, teacher, enemy, or anyone else an incredible letter that will thoroughly brighten that person's day. Include in the letter:

   a. All the things you like about the person (personality characteristics, values, clothes they wear, etc.).

   b. A specific date on which you would like to spend some time with them. This would be great for anybody. Plan to take them shopping or to a movie.

   c. Go though memoryland with them and recount all the fun times you've spent together, and how much they mean to you.

   d. Tell them that you think affirmation is an important part of your relationship, and that you are going to work on being a more encouraging person.

Bible Study

Read each verse below and discuss how it relates to en-
couragement:
Matthew 19:14
1 Thessalonians 5:11
Hebrews 3:13
Hebrews 10:24, 25

Related Scripture

John 13:34, 35   1 Thessalonians 3:12
Romans 12:9-13   1 Timothy 1:5
Romans 13:8   1 Peter 1:22
1 Corinthians 13:4-7

---

1. Quoted by Alan Loy McGinnis, in *The Friendship Factor* (Minne-
apolis: Augsburg Publishing House, 1979), p. 100.

13

CHOOSE TO MAKE
A DIFFERENCE

*S*ome psychologists say that humankind is created only to experience pleasure. I disagree. I believe you and I were created for heroism. Yet, everywhere we look we see people who are so absorbed with their own pain, and who are searching so intently for personal fulfillment, that they rarely bother to notice anyone else's needs.

I once had lunch with a good friend who was going through a crisis in his life. During the conversation I asked how one of our mutual close friends felt about his situation. His reply was unfortunately true for most people: "John is so absorbed with his own pain he hasn't even noticed mine. He means well, but he doesn't have it in him to care, except superficially."

HOW *NOT* TO MAKE A DIFFERENCE

Radically committed Christians must choose to make more of a difference than our mutual friend. They must care about others too much to become guilty of being self-absorbed. They must not argue doctrine that won't matter anyway, for example, while the world bleeds.

On the eve of the Bolshevik Revolution there were two conferences being held in hotels on the same street in Moscow. The Russian Orthodox Church held its national assembly that day, and argued all night about the type of vestments its ministers should wear—while at the other meeting Lenin and friends drew up their final plans to change history for the communist cause.

A church preoccupied with trivia soon becomes blind to the urgent needs of the age. A Christian preoccupied with trivia, pleasure, and self soon becomes impotent in his ability to make a difference in the world.

One of the great religious and political figures of our world was Mahatma Ghandi. When Ghandi studied law in South Africa he attended a Christian church. Ghandi was impressed with Jesus, and thought the Sermon on the Mount was the greatest piece of literature ever put on paper—but he wasn't impressed with Christians. He chided the Christians of his day, and in fact those of us today who take the Lordship of Jesus seriously, when he said that in his judgment the Christian faith does not le,.d itself to much preaching or talking. Instead, it is best propagated by living it and applying it. So Ghandi bluntly asked when Christians would really crown Jesus Christ as the Prince of Peace and proclaim him the champion of the poor and oppressed through our deeds, not just our words.

YOU CAN MAKE A DIFFERENCE

I heard an individual say, "I would rather attempt something great and fail than attempt nothing and succeed." You can make a difference in our world if you attempt something great. You may never become the president of the United States, or speak before millions like Billy Graham. So what? Lives are changed and lives are affected one at a time.

Throughout history God has used everyday people to change the world. The first disciples of Jesus were unassuming, mostly uneducated, untrained men and women who, with a cause to live and die for, took the message of Jesus and changed the world.

Don't let life become a bore. The Christian cause is a reason to live and die. What are you doing with your life right now that is making a small difference in the world?

You might be doing more than you realize. In Alexander Irvin's novel *My Lady of the Chimney Corner*, an old woman went to comfort a neighbor whose boy lay dead. She laid her hand on her friend's head and said,

> Ah, woman. God isn't a printed book to be carried aroun' by a man in fine clothes, not a cross danglin' at the watch chain of a priest. God takes a hand wherever he can find it. Sometimes he takes a Bishop's hand and lays it on a child's head in benediction, the hand of a doctor to relieve pain, the hand of a mother to guide a child, and sometimes he takes the hand of a poor old woman like me to give comfort to a neighbor. But they're all hands touched by His Spirit, and His Spirit is everywhere lookin' for his hands to use.[1]

God's Spirit is looking for hands, bodies, and minds with which to make a difference. But he seldom uses us without our permission. We, like Isaiah, have to say first, "Here am I. Send me" (Isa. 6:8). That is precisely what God wants you to say in order to start your great adventure of service. Some people you know will spend their lives totally self-absorbed and miss the ultimate opportunity—to make a difference in our world.

SERVE GOD IN SIMPLE WAYS

You don't have to give a lot of money to be a leader who

can make a difference for God. You don't have to become a famous missionary. God wants us to serve him where we are and with what we have. Remember Christ's words in Matthew 25?

> Then the righteous will answer him, "Lord, when did we see you hungry and feed you, or thirsty and give you something to drink? When did we see you a stranger and invite you in, or needing clothes and clothe you? When did we see you sick or in prison and go to visit you?" The King will reply, *"I tell you the truth, whatever you did for one of the least of these brothers of mine, you did for me"* (vss. 37-40).

Notice that Jesus mentions the basic necessities of life: food, clothing, and health. Everything he is talking about in Matthew 25 we can do. He isn't talking about bigger-than-life responsibilities, but rather the little things that mean all the difference in the world.

My good friend Terry is a 6'5", 240-pound football player who volunteers to work with the three-year-old Sunday school class at my church. For most of the hour he basically wrestles with these little balls of energy. One day I peeked in the class and saw six little boys climbing all over my massive friend while he laughed and carried them all across the room. Terry doesn't make a big deal out of it, but he is ministering to Jesus as he wrestles those kids.

It's the simple things that make a difference. Sign up to volunteer at a hospital, give away more of your income, teach Sunday school, be a big brother or sister to a needy child. There is so much you can do to be God's instrument for changing lives one by one.

GIVE JUST FOR THE SAKE OF GIVING

True giving has no strings attached. A few years ago I had my income tax statement audited by the government. The woman in charge of my audit was very nice, professional—and skeptical. I walked into her office a little nervous, but sure that I had nothing to hide. She peered at me through her horn-rimmed glasses, and with no formal greeting said, "Mr. Burns, you gave a substantial gift of your income to . . . ," and she named the Christian organization we believe in and support. "Did you give this amount of money?"

She had me intimidated, and I answered with a meek, "Yes."

Then the auditor asked, "What did you receive?"

I now had mustered up my confidence and was a tad bit irritated. I said, "We received nothing but the joy of helping a Christian organization we believe in."

She answered with skepticism in her voice "I'll take your word." Then she added, "There are very few free rides today."

She meant that people today don't give without expecting something in return; and she was partially right. Yet, as you learn the joy of sharing your possessions and money with others, you will experience the joy of giving for the sake of giving.

In Switzerland there is a church called Saint Martin's, named after a Roman soldier who was a Christian. Here's the story about Martin and why this church chose to name itself after this wonderful Christian man.

One cold winter day, as he was entering a city, a beggar stopped him and asked for alms. Martin had no money but the beggar was blue and shivering with cold and Martin gave what he had. He took off his soldier's cloak,

143

worn and frayed as it was; he cut it in two and gave half
of it to the beggar man. That night he had a dream. In it
he saw the heavenly places and all the angels and Jesus
in the midst of them; and Jesus was wearing half a
Roman soldier's cloak. One of the angels said to him,
"Master, why are you wearing that battered old cloak?
Who gave it to you?" And Jesus answered softly, "My
servant Martin gave it to me." [2]

When you give of yourself you are serving Jesus. A saying
of Jesus that was omitted from the Gospels was so important
that the Holy Spirit recalled it for the apostle Paul: "It is more
blessed to give than to receive" (Acts 20:35). Haven't you
ever noticed that givers are happy people?

BE AUTHENTIC

To make a difference in your world you've got to be real.
There is nothing worse than a holier-than-thou Christian who
never shares his hurts and sorrows. Most people can't relate to
perfection; only authentic people make a difference in the
world.

There's an old story about a minister and a soap salesman
who were going for a walk. The salesman was quite a skeptic,
and the two were having an active debate while walking
through a park. The businessman was getting in some good
jabs at the inconsistency of Christians.

Finally the soap salesman asked the minister, "How can
you say that Christianity works when even within the inner
city park you see derelicts of every kind, drugs, pros-
titutes. . . . Then you have the problems of the family, war,
and disease, not to mention the other problems of the world.
How can you say Christianity works? Just look around. It's
not working."

They walked in silence for a few moments. Then the minister turned to his friend and said, "You're a soap salesman right?"

"Yes, of course," was the reply.

"Is it good soap?"

"It's the best soap on the market."

The minister turned and pointed to a small child playing in the park. He was covered with dirt and grime. "This boy is dirty and filthy from the mud in the park," said the minister. "Doesn't your soap help him?"

The salesman said, "Well, you've got to apply the soap."

The minister's response was, "So it is with the Christian faith. You must *apply* the Christian faith in order for it to work."

Authentic Christians, the ones who do not put on a facade, are the ones who make a difference in the world. If you take your faith seriously you don't have to be perfect. You must, however, be real.

I hope you won't settle for anything less than choosing to make a difference in the world. On my desk I keep this phrase in front of me: *I hope you did something of value today. You wasted a whole day if you didn't.*

Disciplines in Discipleship

Things to Think About

1. Who are your heroes?

2. What are your gifts, abilities, and talents that you can use for God?

3. Why is it often easier to settle for second best in life?

4. Has God planted a dream in your heart? If money, time, or age were not a hindrance, what would you want to do with your life?

5. What keeps you from making a greater difference in the world? What holds you back?

Action Steps

1. Pick out a "make a difference" project and decide to *go for it* this week.
2. Ask someone who knows you well what special gifts they see in you, and how you could use those gifts for God.

Group or Family Experience

1. As a group or family, come up with a project to make your community a better place. Brainstorm ideas, pick one, and do it.
2. Go around the room and share this thought: *If nothing could stop me, this is what I would want to do with my life.*
3. Take some time to pray for each other's dreams.

Bible Study

Scripture: Philippians 4:13—*"I can do everything through him who gives me strength."*

1. What does this verse mean?
2. How can we be assured that God will give us strength?
3. How does this verse relate to the dream God has given you to make a difference?

Related Scripture

Proverbs 4:18   Philippians 4:19

2 Corinthians 3:18   Colossians 3:17
Philippians 1:6   1 Peter 2:2, 3

---

1. Alexander Irvine, *My Lady of the Chimney Corner* (Flint, MI: Apple Tree Press, 1981), p. 141.
2. Cited in William Barclay, *The Gospel of Matthew*, in The Daily Study Bible Series (Philadelphia: Westminster Press, 1975) , p. 326.

Why I Sponsor A Child Through Compassion

I can't think of anything more important in life than helping make an impact on the world in which we live by sponsoring a child.

Our family has sponsored a child with Compassion for a number of years. That support of $21 a month - just 70 cents a day - covers the cost for clothing, health care and an education for Ramiro Moises Santi. Our entire family looks forward to receiving Ramiro's letters and we hope to visit him some day.

Recently, I had the opportunity to visit some of Compassion's projects in Ecuador. I came away very impressed that each project is run exclusively by Christians who are committed to giving each child the best possible start in life... and opportunity to receive new life in Jesus Christ.

You , too, can sponsor a deserving boy or girl who needs love, protection, and encouragement.

As a sponsor, you'll receive your child's photo and personal story. You can exchange letters and even send a small amount for gifts on birthdays or at Christmas. Your child will know you by name and appreciate your love, help and prayer.

Won't you join with me in giving a needy child a new start today by completing this coupon or by calling Compassion's toll-free number.

Jim Burns sponsors Ramiro Moises Santi

☐ **YES**, I want to give hope to a child who needs me.

My preference is ☐ Boy ☐ Girl ☐ Either

From: ☐ Any ☐ Africa ☐ Asia ☐ Latin America ☐ Caribbean

Please select a child for my consideration and send me his/her photo, case history and a complete sponsorship packet.

If I wish to begin immediately, I will enclose my first sponsorship check, indicating the amount here:

☐ $21(one month) ☐ $63 (3 months)

Please print: ☐ Mr. ☐ Mrs. ☐ Miss ☐ Ms.

ECFA CHARTER MEMBER

Name_____

Address_____

City_____ State _____Zip_____

Phone_____ Age_____

Sponsorship is tax-deductible and receipts will be sent.

C◉MPASSION
INTERNATIONAL

3955 Cragwood Drive
P.O. Box 7000
Colorado Springs, CO 80933
TOLL FREE: 1-800-336-7676